Tax Breaks for Directors

Indicator

ISBN 978-1-906892-23-4

First Edition - Second print - E01P2

Introduction

Tax Breaks for Directors

Being a company director is an onerous responsibility for which you should be properly compensated. But unless you're a shareholder, how should you go about this in a way that comes with the lowest possible tax bill? Of course, you need to take full advantage of the available tax breaks. Yet how can you find them all? And how can you be sure the Taxman won't come back to ask for more?

This brand new book covers everything from the usual suspects such as salary and dividends to those tax breaks available for working from home to childcare and medical cover.

With a new 50% rate for high earners and restrictions on tax-free personal allowances and higher rate relief on pension contributions now in force, this book brings you right up-to-date on the latest and safest, tax-avoidance strategies. As a result of these changes, reviewing your remuneration package and the tax breaks available to you should have jumped up your "to do" list as a busy director. This book is designed to bring those tax breaks within easy reach.

Martin Attis ACA
Chartered Accountant
Tax Expert

Table of contents

Part 1 - Directors only

Chapter 5 - Company cars

Chapter 6 - Using company assets

Chapter 7 - Loans to directors

Chapter 8 - Medical cover

Chapter 9 - Childcare

Chapter 10 - Expenses

Chapter 11 - Working from home

Chapter 12 - Pension contributions

Chapter 13 - Share schemes

Part 2 - Director/shareholder

Chapter 14 - Dividends

Chapter 15 - Tax-efficient salaries

Chapter 16 - Director's loan account

Chapter 19 - Building up a pension fund

Chapter 20 - Restructuring shares

Chapter 21 - Inheritance Tax breaks

Chapter 22 - Selling your company

Chapter 23 - Year-end planning for directors

Table of contents

PART 1

Directors only

CHAPTER 1

Compensation for being a director

1.1. INTRODUCTION

There are many circumstances where as a director you can be held liable for decisions made by the company, even if you didn't agree with them. In addition, if your company becomes technically insolvent (i.e. its balance sheet shows more liabilities than assets or it can't pay its debts as they fall due), your duties change and you now have to do what you can for the company's creditors, rather than its shareholders. In such circumstances, you might find yourself at the wrong end of a claim to pay your personal money back to the company.

In addition to this, you might find yourself charged with a criminal offence arising out of company business.

As a director of a company, you are taking on an onerous responsibility, and you should be compensated for that.

1.2. WHAT FORM OF COMPENSATION?

Directors' remuneration in company accounts refers to salaries and bonuses paid to directors as senior company employees and forms part of your employment contract with the organisation. The board of directors determines executive remuneration and bonuses. In other words, salary is the reward for the effort of directors who work for the company, rather than those who just own a stake in it, i.e. the shareholders.

By salary we mean the regular pay that you receive as director of your company. Other forms or remuneration, such as having the company pay for your medical insurance or the use of a company car, are an additional part of your package.

Executive compensation is the total remuneration or financial compensation a director receives within a company. This includes a basic salary, any and all bonuses, shares, options, and any other company benefit. Over the past three decades, directors' remmuneration has risen dramatically beyond the level of an average worker's wage. Executive compensation is an important part of corporate governance, and is often determined by a company's board of directors.

It's quite usual these days to offer directors a remuneration package rather than a straight salary. In addition to salary your company might pay certain of your expenses either directly or by reimbursement and provide non-cash benefits.

Here are the basic components of a director's remuneration package:

- a base salary
- short-term incentives, or bonuses
- employee benefits

1

- long-term incentive plans (share schemes)

- termination protection ("Golden Parachute").

Short-term incentives are usually formula-driven and have some performance criteria attached depending on the director's role. For example, the Sales Director's performance-related bonus may be based on growth of turnover; a Managing Director's could be based on profitability. However, these bonuses are often discretionary.

Other components of a director's compensation package may include such perks as a company car, health insurance, using company assets, interest-free loans, generous retirement plans etc. Indeed, once you have negotiated the big salary you are now in a position to give some of it up (sacrificing it) in exchange for more tax-efficient forms of remuneration.

TAX BREAK

Generally, when a company pays your expenses and provides non-cash benefits you have to pay tax as if these items were part of your salary. However, non-cash benefits paid to a director do not give rise to employees' NI contributions.

Directors may also be compensated with shares in the company which are almost always subject to vesting restrictions (a long-term incentive). The vesting term refers to the period of time before the recipient has the right to transfer shares and realise value. To be considered a long-term incentive the period must be in excess of one year (three to five years is common).

TAX BREAK

Cash compensation is taxable on an individual at a high individual rate. If part of that income can be converted to a long-term capital gain, for example by granting share options instead of cash to a director, a more advantageous tax treatment may be obtained by the executive.

Senior directors may enjoy considerable income protection unavailable to many other employees. Often directors receive a Golden Parachute that rewards them substantially if the company gets taken over or they lose their job for other reasons.

1.3. DIRECTORS' FEES

There can be confusion between directors' fees and directors' remuneration. There is a significant difference between the two.

Directors may be paid fees in return for the services provided in governing an organisation, but only if their shareholders approve a resolution to pay them. The board presents what they think is an appropriate pool of fees for the board as a whole to shareholders.

The fees, if approved, represent the upper limit that can be paid to the board. The board then decides how the pool is split between individual directors. Shareholders only have to be approached when the board wants to increase the pool - it's not an annual requirement.

1.4.   TAX RELIEF FOR THE COMPANY

The deductibility of the benefit for company tax purposes must always be considered. This is something that the Taxman will sometimes question. If the provision of the benefit constitutes revenue expenditure there should be no problem in obtaining Corporation Tax relief. This is because it's simply part of the cost of obtaining the director's services within a remuneration package and the expense is, therefore, incurred wholly and exclusively for the purpose of the company's trade.

Where the benefit is provided through capital expenditure, however, the position can be difficult. For the employer to claim capital allowances on the expenditure it has to be on the provision of machinery or plant for the purposes of the trade.

Taking the example of a boat, it's likely that only restricted capital allowances would be claimable to reflect the business aspect. Restricted tax relief for the company (and possibly no relief at all) would not necessarily avoid an income tax charge on the director. Hence, although possible, the tax break for an exotic company purchase may simply not be there.

As with all tax planning, you need to be one step ahead of the Taxman by having documentation to hand to take care of that awkward inspector. That might well include you having a contract of employment with your company. Why?

In order to manage the business a company has to attract and retain key employees. The cost of this usually meets the wholly and exclusively test; provided it's not excessive for the duties performed. Therefore, if you reassess your remuneration package (as an employee) to include a particular expense you would like the company to incur (as a benefit-in kind for yourself), this is, in our opinion, wholly and exclusively for the purposes of the trade too.

However, if challenged on this "part of your remuneration" argument by the Taxman, all you'll need is a copy of what was agreed in writing between you and your company - recorded in company board minutes and as a written addition to your contract of employment.

- as a director of a company you are taking on an onerous responsibility and should be compensated for that
- until you own shares in the company you cannot be compensated for this risk by way of tax-efficient dividends
- before becoming a shareholder you need to concentrate on the tax breaks around having a remuneration package not just a straight salary. Each non-salary component has particular tax breaks associated with it
- if you reassess your remuneration package (as an employee) to include a particular expense you would like the company to incur (as a benefit-in-kind for yourself), the tax deductibility for your company needs to be considered. However, if challenged by the Taxman, all you'll need is a copy of what was agreed in writing between you and your company
- directors' fees are taxed in the same way as a salary would be. So this is not a tax-efficient alternative to salary.

CHAPTER 2

The new higher tax rate regime

2.1. WHAT'S CHANGING?

2.1.1. Income tax changes

£100,000 mark. Since April 6 2010 your personal tax-free allowance is subject to an income limit of £100,000. It is then reduced by £1 for every £2 of adjusted net income above the limit; this is broadly all income after adjustment for pension payments and charitable donations.

£150,000 mark. April 6 2010 also saw the introduction of a new additional income tax rate of 50% for income above £150,000.

Note. Dividend income is currently taxed at 10% where it falls within the basic rate band and 32.5% where liable at the higher rate of tax. A new rate has been introduced for dividends which fall into the income band above £150,000.

Example

The effect of the basic changes from April 6 2010 can be illustrated as follows:

	2009/10		2010/11	
		Tax		Tax
	£	£	£	£
Non-dividend income	200,000		200,000	
Personal allowance	(6,475)		Nil	
Taxable income	193,525		200,000	
Taxable at 20%	37,400	7,480	37,400	7,480
Taxable at 40%	156,125	62,450	112,600	45,040
Taxable at 50%			50,000	25,000
Total tax liability		69,930		77,520

2.1.2. Pension changes

In addition, the government intends to restrict tax relief on pension savings for individuals with taxable income of £150,000 or more. This relief will be tapered down until it's 20%.

Legislation has been introduced to prevent those potentially affected from seeking to forestall this change by increasing their pension savings in excess of their normal irregular pattern, prior to that restriction taking effect.

Broadly, these forestalling measures will apply to individuals with incomes of £150,000 or more who, from April 22 2009, change:

- their normal pattern of regular pension contributions; or
- the normal way in which their pension benefits are accrued; and
- their total pension contributions or benefits accrued exceed generally £20,000 a year.

Care should be taken when making pension contributions if your income breaches the £150,000 limit in any of the three periods 2007/8, 2008/9 or 2009/10. However, the rules are complex so professional advice should be sought.

2.2. WHAT CAN YOU DO ABOUT THIS?

The obvious answer to avoiding these new tax rules is to keep your income below the £100,000/£150,000 limits respectively by looking for ways to avoid, or at least defer, the payment of income tax at the top rate.

The potential tax-saving options available to directors may seem overwhelming in their incentives, but it's crucial for you to seek professional advice prior to taking any action as HMRC regularly announce anti-avoidance legislation to mitigate any schemes which they deem as tax avoidance.

Some of the effects on high earning directors and the measurers which may be considered to mitigate their exposure to the new higher rate are as follows.

2.2.1. Timing of payments

As directors are generally taxed on their employment income, dividends and interest from investments on a cash-received basis, one simple way of tax planning is to consider the timing of such payments.

Deferring the tax charge. You may seek to delay increases in salary if you believe the new rate is only a temporary measure by the present government.

Spreading the tax charge. Option schemes can be amended to allow directors greater flexibility over the time at which they are required to exercise their options. This may assist those directors who hold options whose exercise would otherwise result in the employee moving into a higher tax band.

2.2.2. Salary sacrifices

High earning directors may increasingly seek the option from their employer to exchange part of their salary or pension contributions for other tax-free benefits such as childcare vouchers or share schemes.

However, HMRC has already announced it will seek to negate the benefit of such salary sacrifice schemes for anyone earning in excess of £150,000.

Such schemes will be of particular interest to directors earning between £100,000 and £150,000. From 2011, these directors will lose their personal tax allowances but will still be able to obtain the higher rate relief on pension contributions.

Accordingly, if they are able to make a higher pension contribution and reduce their salary below £100,000, they will qualify for full tax relief on their pension contributions whilst keeping their personal allowances intact. For those earning between £100,000 and £112,950, pension contributions sufficient to reduce their income to less than £100,000 give an effective marginal rate of tax saving at 60%.

2.2.3. Inter-spouse transfers

Gifting assets between husband and wife has long been an efficient way of mitigating Inheritance Tax and Capital Gains Tax liabilities. Now, however, you should consider gifting income-generating assets to your spouse if they are lower rate taxpayers. It may also be appropriate to fund contributions to your spouse's pension scheme.

2.2.4. Pension contributions

At the same time as introducing the new higher rate of income tax, the Chancellor simultaneously announced anti-forestalling legislation to prevent higher rate taxpayers from taking excessive advantage of the tax relief on pension contributions (see 2.1.2).

However, high earning directors should not be discouraged from making contributions if they are carefully considered as there may still be some benefit to be gained under the transitional provisions in place both this year and next. For example, those earning more than £150,000 can benefit from contributions made up to £20,000 for the current and following tax years.

2.2.5. Delivering capital instead of income

The changes in income tax and NI rates will make it significantly more tax efficient to receive rewards in the form of capital gains (currently taxed at 18%) rather than income. There are several well established ways of achieving this for companies and their directors.

For example:

- private companies may be able to create performance shares taxed at the hands of their directors on their initial (in most cases low) value, but which grow if the company is successful and can be sold with the increase in value being taxed as a capital gain

- the changes in tax and NI rates also make approved share schemes more attractive for many directors. Companies should review their current arrangements to ensure that these tax-favoured schemes are being used to maximum effect. Some employers are using approved options as part of whole share incentive awards to improve tax efficiency awards to senior executives.

2.2.6. Gift Aid donations and charitable giving

It is not currently clear how the new higher rate of tax will interact with the mechanism of Gift Aid relief for charitable donations.

Tax relief is given on gifts by reducing an individual's taxable income by the market value of the asset. The potential tax saving would therefore be at 50% to the extent that the market value of the gift exceeds your taxable income.

KEY POINT

- high-income directors need to consider their options carefully as each of their circumstances will be different and there is no single solution to avoiding the new higher rates for 2010/11. It's essential that you seek professional advice before taking any action or face the risk of incurring unexpected tax liabilities.

CHAPTER 3

Your salary

3.1. INTRODUCTION

By salary we mean the regular pay that you receive as director of your company, rather than other forms of remuneration, such as having the company pay for your medical insurance.

In other words, salary is the reward for the effort of directors who work for the company, rather than those who just own a stake in it, i.e. the shareholders. So if you are just a shareholder and do no work for the company you can't strictly have a salary that the company gets a tax deduction for. You can, however, be paid a dividend.

3.2. SALARY

In principle you can have as much pay as you want. There's no official cap on the amount you can be paid as a director, however, there is the National Minimum Wage to consider. This will apply if you are legally treated as a worker employed by your company but may not if you only act as a company director or company secretary.

TAX BREAK

For 2010/11 the first £6,475 (£539.55 per month) of your salary will be free of income tax and the first £5,720 (£476.67) of this is also NI-free.

Your salary as a director should have most of the tax due deducted under the PAYE system before you receive it. Obviously, the more salary you take the more tax you will pay, so the level of salary is important if you do not want to pay too much tax.

On the other hand, withdrawing no pay at all is not ideal either because it can restrict the amount of tax-deductible pension contributions you can make and affect your entitlement to certain social security benefits and State Pension.

Your company will also benefit from you taking out some salary, as the pay you will take will reduce profits and the amount of tax paid on them.

For your director's salary to be tax deductible for the company, your rate of pay must not be excessive in relation to the work done; for example paying a part-time director £40,000 per year just for attending four board meetings. The Taxman may argue that the reward does not reflect the work done, so the payment is not tax deductible for the company.

3.3. £50K PLUS SALARIES

From a trawl of recent job ads we have plumped for an example salary of £75,000, to illustrate how much tax and NI you'd end up paying over a whole tax year. So what would be your take home pay on £75,000?

1. Your income tax bill for 2009/10 should have been:

FOR A WHOLE TAX YEAR	£	INCOME TAX BILL (£)
Gross salary	75,000	
Tax-free amount	(6,475)	
Taxable salary	68,525	
Taxed at 20%	37,400	7,480
Taxed at 40%	31,125	12,450
		19,930

2. Your NI bill is then:

FOR A WHOLE TAX YEAR	£	NI BILL (£)
Gross salary	75,000	
NI-free amount	(5,720)	
Taxable salary	69,280	
NI at 11%	38,168	4,198
NI at 1%	31,112	311
		4,509

3. Leaving you a net salary of:

GROSS SALARY	INCOME TAX DEDUCTED	NI DEDUCTED	NET SALARY
£75,000	£19,930	£4,509	£50,561
100%	26.57%	6.01%	67.42%

That's £4,213 net salary per month out of a gross monthly salary of £6,250.

3.4. WHAT TO PUT ON YOUR TAX RETURN?

Your salary is income from an employment so you should complete the "Employment" pages on your tax return. If you receive salary (or director's fees) from more than one company, you should complete a separate set of "Employment" pages for each company.

The amount of your salary for a particular tax year is the total figure of earnings from employment shown on a Form P60, which you should receive from the company by May 31 each year. To complete your tax return (tick the box for director) copy the figures of pay and tax deducted from the P60 in the appropriate boxes on the tax return "Employment" pages. You do not have to copy the amount of employees' NI you have paid on your salary.

3.4.1. Deductible expenses

In order to deduct expenses from your salary the costs must be wholly, exclusively and necessarily incurred in the performance of your work. This is a very strict test and does not cover expenses incurred to put you in a better position to perform your duties, such as the cost of travelling to work. Allowable expenses include:

Professional subscriptions. Members of professions may deduct the cost of fees and subscriptions paid to their professional bodies that they are required to belong to as a condition of their employment. The Taxman keeps a list of these approved bodies, see http://www.hmrc.gov.uk/kust3/index.htm

Business mileage and parking. If you use your car for business and the company pays you less than the tax-free rate (40p per mile for the first 10,000 miles and 25p thereafter) you can claim the difference. Plus you can claim any parking fees (not fines though) associated with a business journey that your company did not reimburse you for.

Both of these can be claimed through the "Employment" pages of your tax return.

3.5. HOW MUCH TAX WILL YOU PAY?

The rate at which you have income tax and NI deducted from your salary in 2010/11 will depend on your total income and PAYE code:

Tax and NI

INCOME TAX RATES	£	
Basic rate	0 to 37,400	20%
Higher rate	37,401 to 150,000	40%
Additional rate	Over 150,000	50%

ANNUAL	TAX RATE	TAX ON THIS SLICE OF INCOME
Personal tax-free allowance £6,475*	0%	-
On next £37,400	20%	£7,480
On next £112,600	40%	+40p in the £
Above this	50%	+50p in the £

*   Where your taxable income exceeds £100,000, the personal tax-free allowance is reduced by £1 for every £2 over that amount.

ANNUAL NI	NI RATE	NI ON THIS SLICE OF INCOME
On first £5,720	0%	-
On next £38,168	11%	
Above £43,888	1%	

3.5.1. PAYE codes

Your salary as a director should have most of the tax due deducted under the PAYE system before you receive it. However, if your total income has suddenly increased or the PAYE code during the tax year was incorrect for any reason, e.g. a benefit-in-kind was missing, you may have some additional tax to pay on your tax return.

The additional tax will be paid on January 31 following the end of the tax year, which is also the final date for submitting your tax return. The additional tax due will be included within your PAYE code for the following tax year (say, 2010/11), as long as the amount due is less than £2,000. This means you do not have to find the cash on January 31, as it will be collected through your code. The catch is you have to submit your tax return early enough for this to be possible.

DO = higher rate tax
K = benefits greater than tax code. Max. of £50 a month can be taken.

KEY POINTS

- most of the tax and NI for a given tax year will have been paid upfront under the PAYE system, meaning you don't have to find the money later
- a salary pushes up the maximum amount of pension contribution you are allowed to pay into a personal pension or company scheme. If you are near retirement age your salary can also maximise the amount of pension you will receive from a company pension scheme
- if you receive a salary from the company you will be entitled to receive certain State benefits
- in addition to income tax, your gross salary (over £5,720) will be subject to NI for both you as a private individual and your company
- there are only a very few limited expenses which can be deducted from your salary income.

CHAPTER 4

Directors' bonuses

4.1. INTRODUCTION

A director's bonus is paid in addition to salary as a special reward for work done. How much usually depends on how much profit the company has made.

Directors/shareholders are rewarded with dividends rather than bonuses. Many directors may also be shareholders, so it's always important to distinguish whether an amount paid to a director is a bonus or a dividend. The tax treatment is quite different.

The rules of most companies, the Articles of Association, require the shareholders to agree remuneration paid to a director, usually by voting on a resolution approving the sum to be paid for the year. However, in practice salary and bonuses are paid to directors before this meeting happens.

In principle, there's no cap on the level of bonus you can have. Obviously the larger the bonus the more tax you will pay, as your total income for the year will be higher. So the level of your bonus is important if you prefer not to pay too much tax. The payment of a large bonus also attracts NI for both you and your company.

The money paid as a bonus can often be taken out of the company in different forms. If a large bonus is taken out, there will be less money available to reward you in other, possibly more tax efficient, ways.

The date of the bonus is key. In principle, a bonus is always deductible for the company, as it's an expense wholly and exclusively incurred by the company for the purposes of its trade.

4.2. WHAT TO PUT ON YOUR TAX RETURN?

Your bonus is part of your income from employment so you should complete the "Employment" pages on your return. A bonus is taxable in the year in which it is awarded or paid out.

The amount of your bonus should be included in the total figure of earnings from employment shown on the Form P60, which you should receive from the company by May 31 each year. To complete your tax return (tick the box for director) copy the figures of pay and tax deducted from the P60 in the appropriate boxes on the tax return "Employment" pages. You do not have to copy the amount of employees' NI you have paid on your bonus and salary.

If you have a special non-taxable bonus, such as a payment from a staff suggestion scheme, you don't have to include it on your tax return.

4.3. WHAT'S THE NI COST?

If you are already paying NI at 1% on the top slice of your salary, then this is the rate you'll pay on your cash bonus. Your company should deduct all the NI due from your bonus before the amount is paid to you. If a mistake has been made in the calculations, the Taxman will ask the company to pay any additional NI due.

4.4. AT WHAT RATE WILL YOUR BONUS BE TAXED?

It depends. Your director's bonus is taxed just like your salary, so the final amount of tax you pay on it will depend on the level of your total income for the year in which the bonus is awarded or paid. The full amount of tax due under PAYE should have been deducted by the company and paid over to the Taxman before you receive the net amount.

However, if the PAYE code used was incorrect for any reason, the tax due on your bonus may be more than the tax deducted under PAYE. In this case there will be some additional tax due, which will show up when you submit your tax return. If this sum is less than £2,000, the Taxman will adjust your PAYE code for the next year to collect all the tax due gradually. He can only do this if your tax return is submitted early. If you wait until January 31, the Taxman will not have time to adjust your PAYE code, which is sent out in February, to be used from April 5.

If more than £2,000 additional tax is due, it must be paid by the January 31 following the end of the tax year, which is also the final date for submitting your return.

INCOME TAX RATES	£	
Basic rate	0 to 37,400	20%
Higher rate	34,701 to 150,000	40%
Additional rate (from 2010)	Over 150,000	50%

	BONUS (£)	INCOME TAX (£)	NI (£)	NET (£)	%
Basic rate	10,000	2,000	1,100	6,900	69
Higher rate	10,000	4,000	100	5,900	59
Additional rate	10,000	5,000	100	4,900	49

4.5. DEFERRING A BONUS

With the new higher rates of income tax of 50% for those earning in excess of £150,000, high income directors will be looking for ways to avoid or at least defer; the payment of income tax at the top rate.

The potential tax-saving options available to directors may seem overwhelming in their incentives but it is crucial for you to seek professional advice prior to taking any action as HMRC are regularly announcing anti-avoidance legislation to mitigate any schemes which they deem as tax avoidance.

Two examples of the measurers which may be considered to mitigate your exposure to the new higher rate are as follows:

4.5.1. Deferring the tax charge

One way to defer the charge is by making loans backed by a deferred bonus or some other incentive. A modest benefit-in-kind charge will arise in the year in which the loan is outstanding (assuming interest is not paid by the director).

The downside to this planning is that tax rates may remain high for a sufficiently long period that the yearly benefit-in-kind charges outweigh the saving on the headline rate of tax. Conversely, you may believe the new rate is only a temporary measure by the present government.

4.6. AN ALTERNATIVE TO CASH

Cash bonus payments may be a bit thin on the ground for anyone who isn't a banker. Hard pressed companies, struggling to meet existing commitments, may balk at the prospect of parting with their cash. However, there may be better ways of approaching the situation.

Distribute profits as a bonus to selected directors or in the form of pension scheme contributions and other benefits. Indeed, a bonus may also be paid by transferring the ownership of an existing company asset, such as shares or a car. Or you could leave the bonus within your company, so that the company credits your after-tax amount to your director's current account. You then draw it from the company as it can afford to pay you.

- use performance-related bonuses to allow you to receive more remuneration and the company's reduce taxable profits when times are good (and vice versa)
- the obligation to pay a bonus must be recorded before the year-end. Tax and NI on a bonus provided in the year-end accounts must be paid within nine months from the end of the accounting period
- distribute profits as a bonus to selected directors or in the form of pension scheme contributions and other benefits.

CHAPTER 5

Company cars

5.1.　INTRODUCTION

Of all the fringe benefits of being a director the company car is still the most popular. Indeed, if a company is looking for staff at director level they will find that they have to offer a car as part of the remuneration package. One of the attractions of having a car provided by your company is the tax treatment.

The car benefit figure is supposed to cover the benefits associated with the provision of the car such as insurance, road tax, repairs, and maintenance payments, but this is not reduced if the director meets any of those expenses. So don't contribute to running expenses!

TAX BREAK 1

Tax is payable according to a scale charge (depending on the car's CO_2 emissions rating), which in most cases does not reflect the true value to you of having the car, particularly if you would have to finance the acquisition of your own car.

TAX BREAK 2

Another advantage is that the car benefit does not count as "earnings" for NI purposes. You do not pay NI on the cash equivalent value of the company car. Only the company has to pay NI on this benefit-in-kind. So even directors don't pay employees' NI on a company car.

5.2.　THE CAR ITSELF

The car should be owned or leased by the company and lent to you to use as you wish. The company should insure the vehicle for both business and pleasure use, and pay for the car tax, plus all repair and servicing costs. You should not take on the ownership of the car, although you can be its registered keeper.

If you sign a lease agreement in your name, but the company pays the instalments on your behalf, it's not a company car. In this case you are financially responsible for it as the lease is in your name.

5.2.1.　Does it matter what type of car you have?

You are taxed on the so-called cash equivalent of the benefit of having a company car. The cash equivalent is calculated as a percentage of the car's list price for every year or part of a year in which you can use it. The percentage of the list price used depends on the official CO_2 emissions figure for the car, which is fixed at the time of manufacture and is shown on the vehicle's registration document (V5) for cars registered since March 1 2001.

The list price is the price that a single car would have been sold at in the UK on the day before it was first registered, not what the company actually paid for it. This price does not include any discounts given by a dealer, but it should include the cost of any extras worth over £100 that are added at any time. The list price of a car can generally be checked on the manufacturer's website.

5.3.   WHAT TO PUT ON YOUR TAX RETURN?

The company car is a benefit from your employment with the company so you should complete the "Employment" pages of your tax return. The cash equivalent value of the company car must be included in the section headed "Benefits and Expenses". The figure to use will be shown on the annual Return of Expenses and Benefits (Form P11D) completed by the company for you each tax year. The company has to give you a copy of Form P11D or a list of the entries included on it by July 6 each year.

You do not pay tax on the company car before it's made available to you. The tax due on the cash equivalent value of it should be deducted from your salary gradually through the PAYE system while you are using the car.

However, if you were provided with a company car late during the tax year, or the amount of cash equivalent value for the car included in your tax code was incorrect, there may be more tax to pay. If the additional tax due is more than £2,000 it must be paid by January 31 after the end of the tax year. If it's less than £2,000 and you submitted your tax return in good time, the extra tax will be collected through the PAYE system in the following tax year.

TIP

You should, however, check your PAYE notice of coding to ensure that the cash equivalent value of your company car has been included. You should also check that the amount shown is correct. It is not unknown for the Taxman to make an error.

The car benefit charge does not cover the provision of private fuel; a chauffeur, or driver expenses such as fines, tolls and parking costs. There is a separate benefit charge for taxing the provision of fuel for private travel, which is considered below. In cases where the company provides a chauffeur or pays for a driver's costs, the employee is taxed on the full cost incurred by the company.

5.4. MAKING A CONTRIBUTION

5

Company cars

Tax break

You could make a contribution to the cost of the car. This is knocked off the list price, to a maximum of £5,000, before the car benefit is calculated. The tax on the benefit-in-kind is reduced each year you continue to use the company car.

Example

Say you want a mid-range car, with CO_2 emissions of 205g/km. Each year you would be charged tax equal to the car's original list price multiplied by 30%. On a capital contribution of £5,000 you will reduce the benefit charge by £1,500 (£5,000 x 30%). At a top rate of tax at 50% this saves you £750. If you keep the same car for four years, that's £3,000.

Because your car benefit is reduced, so is your company's corresponding NI. It will save £192 per year (at current NI rates). Over four years that's £768.

5.5. OPTIONAL EXTRAS

The tax payable on company cars is calculated from a combination of how much CO_2 it emits and its original list price. The higher the emissions, the greater the percentage of the list price is treated as a benefit-in-kind (BiK). This includes the cost of any extras fitted, such as sat nav.

Example

Simon decides his four-year-old car needs replacing. He's looking at a similar model costing £20,000 with CO_2 emissions of 210g/km. The taxable benefit is 30% of the list price, i.e. £5,800. But Simon decides to treat himself to the manufacturer's fitted "entertainment pack". This adds £2,000 to the list price and another £600 to the taxable benefit (£2,000 x 30%).

So when you add, say, sat nav as an extra to your company car, it will cost you more in tax. However, there's a way to reduce or even eliminate this extra tax bill.

Tax break

The Taxman won't charge tax on extras with a list price totalling £100 or less, but that's not going to get you much these days. However, there's an exemption that's often overlooked. There's no tax on extras if they're to be used for the business. The Taxman gives an example of a tow-bar that's used to pull a trailer for carrying equipment.

Tip

Tip

If your job means that you drive to many different locations, it's fair to say that sat nav could be useful. It can therefore be excluded from the BiK tax charge. Make sure that whoever is preparing your Forms P11D is aware of any extras that need to be excluded from the list price of the car.

Tax break

It's difficult to justify a tax exemption for a DVD player as an extra on the basis that it's necessary for your business. But even if you can't avoid a tax charge, there's a way you can reduce the amount payable. The cost of extras is only added to the list price of the car if they are fixed to the vehicle. So a DVD player, or any other accessory that isn't fitted in the car, won't be charged to tax under the same rules. Instead, the BiK is calculated at a flat rate of 20% of the cost of the extra.

Example

Assume the same facts as the example above, but instead of adding the manufacturer's options Simon purchases separate DVD and sat nav systems that are detachable. These cost him the same amount as the built-in ones - £2,000. But he'll now pay tax on a benefit-in-kind of only £400 (£2,000 x 20%).

Warning. Some cars have a BiK rate of less than 20%. If this is the case, then adding fitted extras will cost less in tax than detachable versions.

Tip

The tax payable on a detachable extra for your car is based on what your company pays for it, rather than the original list price. That's useful in today's market because there are some good discounts to be had if you shop around.

Employers' NI contributions are due on BiK at 12.8%. So if you can reduce the BiK charge on a car accessory, not only will you save tax but your company can also cut its NI costs.

5.6. CAR FUEL BENEFIT

If you are provided with petrol (or other fuel) for private motoring, you will be taxed on this benefit by reference to another scale charge: £18,000 (£16,900 for 2009/10) x benefit percentage (combination of list price and CO_2 emissions).

You can avoid the fuel benefit charge by paying for all the private motoring yourself and records are kept to prove this should the Taxman come to call.

In deciding whether it's beneficial for your company to pay for fuel for private motoring it's necessary to consider:

- the amount of the scale charge
- the number of private miles travelled
- the car's fuel consumption
- the price of fuel
- the director's income tax rate.

Example

The company Mercedes C280 Sport has CO_2 emissions of 219g/km and had a list price of £31,077 when acquired. For driving the Mercedes C280 Sport in 2009/10 you would be taxed on £9,633 (31% x £31,077) for the car and £5,239 (31% x £16,900) for the free fuel provided. This amounts to a total tax charge of £5,948 ((£9,633 + £5,239) x 40%).

Example

The company Mercedes C280 Sport has CO_2 emissions of 219g/km and had a list price of £31,077 when acquired. It does 30.7 miles per gallon according to its technical specification. Your tax charge in 2010/11 for free fuel is £2,232 (40% x (31% x £18,000)). If the cost of petrol were, say, £1.10 per litre (£4.95 per gallon), even in the supermarket garages this would buy 451 gallons of fuel to drive 13,486 miles. If you drive more than 13,486 private miles in 2010/11, you're quids in. If you expect to drive fewer miles on non-business related journeys, cut out the free fuel.

5.6.1. Reducing the tax bill

TIP 1

If your private mileage is expected to be less than the break-even point for your car, buy all the fuel yourself and get the company to pay you a fuel-only mileage rate for all business-related journeys. The Taxman has set advisory fuel rates for different fuel types and engine sizes, which can be paid tax-free without quibble. The Mercedes C280 has a 2,996cc engine, so the company can pay you 19p per mile tax-free for business journeys.

5.7.   SECOND COMPANY CAR

Let's say one of your dependants needs a car. You would like to help but if you give them the money it will be after you have paid tax and NI at, say, 41%, which makes it expensive for you. They don't work for your company and so wouldn't be entitled to a company car in their own right. However, would it be tax effective for you to have two company cars but let them use one?

TAX BREAK

A second company car is a cheaper way of providing a vehicle to another member of your family than drawing the money out of the company and financing it yourself, particularly if the car has a low CO_2 emissions rating.

If a second company-owned car is made available for private use as part of your remuneration package, the company can pay for all the repairs, running costs and even the insurance, and claim Corporation Tax relief on these expenses as well as the car itself. The catch is a benefit-in-kind charge on you for the second car. So how much tax will this cost you?

In recent years we've seen a steady increase in the level of taxation on company cars, so that the tax cost is now prohibitively high; generally, the advice has been not to provide second company cars.

The taxable benefit of company cars is based on their CO_2 emissions ratings. The lower the rating, the lower the percentage of list price used to calculate the taxable benefit. It starts at 15% for cars with up to 135g/km and increases by 1% for each 5g/km thereafter up to a 35% maximum.

For example, if your company spends £8,835 on a car (which has a CO_2 emissions of 127g/km) and makes this available for private use by your son or daughter, the tax cost to you as a benefit-in-kind would be as follows:

£8,835 x 15% = £1,325.25 taxable on you at 40% = £530.10. That's the cost of the car plus all its running costs for just over £500! The savings can be greater for more expensive cars.

If the second car arrives as a present in, say, July, the tax cost for 2010/11 will be even less because the car will have only been available for just nine months of the tax year (for example, July 6 2010 to April 5 2011).

Obviously your company has to pay for the financing and running costs of the car. However, this is going to work out cheaper from a tax point of view than drawing the money out of your company, paying tax on that and using the net of tax amount to fund the car personally.

The company will have to pay employers' NI at 12.8% on the value of this car benefit.

Your company would also get a 100% tax deduction for the cost of the car if it has an emissions rating of 110g/km or less.

TIP

To avoid any quibble with the Taxman, have this second car recorded as part of your remuneration package with the company. It's tax deductible for the company on the grounds of being wholly and exclusively necessary for the company to keep its key member of staff happy.

5.8. A CLASSIC CAR

Your existing company car is functional but not much fun to drive at the weekend. Two company cars are one answer, but doesn't that also double your tax bill?

TAX BREAK

Get your company to provide you with a "classic" (worth less than £15,000) as your second company car. With its minimal tax cost, this is worth doing.

If you do a large number of business miles, the last thing you'll want to do in your spare time is get back into that company car again. However, if your company paid for it, you might think differently about using a second, more attractive, car for cruising at the weekend. But aren't there rules that make sure you pay tax on such a perk?

If a company car is more than 15 years old, and its value is more than £15,000, the rules cancel out the tax advantage of having a "classic car". In this instance, instead of the list price, it's the market value you have to use. For example, take a classic car with a market value of £20,000. At the maximum car tax charge of

35%, the taxable benefit-in-kind of the car made available by your company for your private use is £7,000 (35% x £20,000), on which your company would pay employers' NI of £896 (12.8% x £7,000). As a higher rate taxpayer your income tax bill goes up by £2,800 (40% x £7,000). Not so nice wheels!

What about cars that are not worth £15,000? For example, an E-type Jaguar dating from the mid-to-late 1960s might have had a list price of £2,000 then, but the current market value is not quite up to the magic £15,000 figure. For details on how much classic cars cost take a look at http://www.classic-car-directory.com/price. asp This car can be driven to your heart's content on the company and still only give rise to a maximum tax charge of 35% of the list price. At a list price of £2,000, this is a scale charge of only £700 (35% x £2,000), and tax of £280 (40% x £700) for a higher rate taxpayer. No bad for, say, five figures of private mileage.

TIP

To significantly reduce your tax bill choose a "classic" as your second company car with a market value of less than £15,000 (with a low original list price). You then get to drive your private miles in a beautiful car - all expenses paid (by your company).

TIP

Pay for your own fuel, otherwise you'll be hit for a car fuel scale charge. At a maximum of 35% of the fixed fuel benefit figure of £18,000 for 2010/11, there's a potential benefit-in-kind which far outweighs the car.

5.9.   4X4 PICK-UP

If your company makes a car or a van available to you for your private use (i.e. any non-business journey excluding ordinary commuting), then there is a benefit-in-kind. For a company van provided between April 6 2006 and April 5 2007 it's a flat £3,000. For a car in the same period, it's a percentage of its list price - ranging from 35% down to 15%. If you were a 40% taxpayer, how much would you pay in tax?

Typically (although there are exceptions) a 4x4 is not a van but "just a car". So as a 40% taxpayer, a £30,000 4x4 will cost you around £4,200 (£30,000 x 35% x 40%) a year in real money, plus the usual 12.8% NI charge for the company.

A pick-up on the other hand, is not a car but a van. So for an equivalent pick-up it's only £1,200 a year in tax (£3,000 x 40%) and £153.60 in employers' NI (£3,000 x 12.8%). The pick-up doesn't have to be a utilitarian builder's wagon. In fact, these vehicles can be quite luxurious. Currently, the Taxman doesn't question what use you put the vehicle to. You don't have to justify the pick-up as an integral part of your business any more than you would have to with a van.

There is an additional £500 if fuel for private journeys is also provided. However, for a car it's a fixed £18,000 (for 2010/11) x a percentage ranging from 35% down to 15%.

For those with a top of the range pick-up, being taxed at the van rate (including fuel) is more tax effective than the tax you'd pay on an equivalent spend (and emissions-rated) company car.

Unfortunately, there's little point in trying to swing an insignificant private use category on your personal pick-up. For example, he'll only let you make one trip to the tip each year. A bit mean this Taxman.

KEY POINTS

- when the company provides you with a car all the hassle of car ownership is removed. You don't have to worry about servicing, the cost of repairs or insurance. The company also takes on the burden of a loan or lease to acquire the car, and will supply a replacement when you need one
- you don't have to pay NI on the cash equivalent value of the company car, although you do pay income tax on that amount
- the company must pay employers' NI at 12.8% on the cash equivalent value of the company car
- the value of the cash equivalent, which is the amount you pay tax on, may be greater than the cost of providing the car
- the company can provide members of your family or household with company cars to use as they wish. You will be taxed on the cash equivalent value of those cars, but it can be more tax-efficient for the company to provide small, fuel-efficient cars, rather than pay you extra salary to buy those cars personally
- when the company incurs the expense of a company car it reduces the profits subject to Corporation Tax, particularly if the car has an official CO_2 emissions figure of 110g/km or less
- if the tax you would pay on free fuel is less than the cost of the fuel used for your private journeys, take the free fuel. But you need to recalculate this break-even point for the new tax cost from April 6 2010
- the company can pay you a tax-free mileage rate for using the company car for business-related journeys, if it does not also provide you with free fuel for those journeys
- use up to £5,000 of this rate to contribute to the cost of a company car to reduce the benefit-in-kind tax. It could save useful amounts on income tax and employers' NI over four years
- if you use your sat nav, or other car accessory, for businesss, you won't be liable to pay tax on it as a benefit-in-kind. And even where it is taxable, you can cut tax and your company's NI bill by using a detachable version.
- If a pick-up suits your lifestyle, get your company to provide you with one rather than an equivalent car
- the cash equivalent value of free fuel provided for private use in a company car is very high. It will not be tax-efficient to have free fuel provided by the company unless you drive a higher than average number of non-business-related miles during the year.

CHAPTER 6

Using company assets

6.1. INTRODUCTION

If an asset is sold to a director at a price that is less than its market value, the director receives a taxable benefit equal to the difference. What some employers do instead is to put assets such as furniture, expensive suits etc. at the disposal of the director.

If instead of being bought, the asset is rented, the amount of rent is assessable.

Once having been used, if the asset is then transferred to the director, the benefit at that time is based on the greater of:

- the open market value at the time of the transfer; and
- the market value at the time it was first used by the director less the amounts assessed for tax while being used.

The company can buy an asset, say a computer or a hi-fi, and let you use it in your own home with no restriction.

6

Using company assets

> **TAX BREAK**
>
> Instead of being taxed on the full value of an asset if the company gave it to you, you only pay tax on 20% of the value each tax year. That's market value at the time it was first put at your disposal. If your family also uses the asset, there's no additional tax charge.

> **TAX BREAK**
>
> You don't have to pay employees' NI on the cash equivalent of the asset provided.

The company should purchase the asset in its own name, retain ownership, insure and maintain it. If the company gives you the asset, you will be taxed as if you had received a bonus equal to its market value on the date it was transferred.

The tax you pay is based on the value of the asset. The higher the value, the more tax there is to pay.

Warning. If the company pays for additional services which allow you to use the asset, such as an Internet connection or mooring fees for a boat, you will also be taxed on the cost of such services. So keep an eye on these too.

6.2. WHAT TO PUT ON YOUR TAX RETURN?

The cash equivalent value as shown on your Form P11D must be reported on your tax return on the "Employment" pages under the heading "Benefits and Expenses".

If the provision of the asset is not taxable, such as a computer, you don't have to enter anything on your tax return.

Any money you pay to the company in return for using the asset can reduce the amount you are taxed on. This is known as making good.

You don't pay tax on the provision of the asset before it is made available to you. Any tax due on the cash equivalent value of the asset should be deducted from your salary every month under the PAYE system. This is after your tax code has been updated by the Taxman for this benefit-in-kind.

6.3.   EXAMPLES OF USING COMPANY ASSETS

6.3.1.   Antiques

Example

In 2009/10 Centurion Ltd made available an antique dining room table and chairs to Michael, the managing director, and a painting to Giles, the sales director. The table and chairs were worth £4,000 in 2009/10 and £5,000 when they were sold to Michael in 2011/12 for £2,000. The painting was worth £3,000 in 2009/10 and £1,200 when it was sold to Giles in 2011/12.

	MICHAEL		GILES	
Assessable benefits	*£*	*£*	*£*	*£*
2009/10 20% x market value	*800*		*600*	
2010/11 20% x market value	*800*		*600*	
2011/12 greater of:				
Market value when transferred	*5,000*	*5,000*	*1,200*	
Market value when first used	*4,000*		*3,000*	
Less benefits already assessed	*1,600*		*1,200*	
	2,400		*1,800*	*1,800*
Less amount paid by directors		*2,000*		*800*
		3,000		*1,000*
Director's income tax at 40%		*1,200*		*400*

6.3.2.   Smartphones

At some point the Taxman started to worry that companies were giving bonuses in the form of tax-free widescreen televisions, MP3 players and other electrical luxuries. Because they could be bundled up with the company's computer equipment (but used for personal reasons) a tax charge was being avoided.

He then moved his attention on to company-provided BlackBerrys and other personal digital assistants (PDAs) which had been exempt from tax because they were used mainly as mobile telephones. However, they do have additional functions more typically associated with a computer. So could a director who sends too many personal e-mails on a work PDA potentially face a bill of hundreds of pounds?

TAX BREAK

The level of your private usage of computer-related equipment provided to you by your company will not be the deciding factor. If it's made available in order to carry out your duties of employment in the first place, then you're unlikely to be taxed on its private use. You'll need a copy of the written company policy governing the issue of each "device".

6.3.3. Home computing

Directors who already had the benefit of an employer-funded computer before April 6 2006 can continue to enjoy tax-free use of the equipment until it comes to be replaced. An "upgrade" of component parts would also technically bring the exemption to an end.

TAX BREAK

If there's insignificant private use of the computer, you don't have to make an entry on the director's P11D for computers issued on or after April 6 2006. This is provided your company has: **(1)** a company policy on private use; and **(2)** recorded its decision that recovering the costs of private use is impractical.

6.3.4. Other "out of office" items

Your company has to calculate the cash equivalent value of you having the use of any asset, unless it's covered by an exemption, such as a mobile phone. The Taxman says this value is equal to 20% of the asset's market value "when first provided to you", plus any other costs the company incurs in providing the asset.

Example

If the company purchases a new blu ray DVD player for £822 and immediately "lends" it to you to use at home, you are taxed on the cash equivalent value of £164 (£822 x 20%) for every year that you have use of the DVD player. If the company provides you with an older player that costs £294 new but is now worth only £60 when you start to use it, you're taxed on the cash equivalent value of £12 per year (£60 x 20%).

6

TAX BREAK

The annual cash equivalent value can be reduced if the company uses the asset for a little while before lending it to you, i.e. so that it depreciates in value.

TAX BREAK

If the asset is only available for you to use for part of the year, the cash equivalent value can be reduced in proportion to the length of time during which you could use the asset. To get this reduction past the Taxman, you will need documentation such as board minutes and a clause in your contract of employment that restricts the availability of the asset.

TAX BREAK

If the asset is used exclusively for your business at certain times, the cash equivalent value is reduced by the proportion that represents the business use.

Example

If the company provides you with a combined printer/copier/scanner machine which costs £588, but 70% of your use of the machine is to do with company business, the taxable cash equivalent value will be £35 per year; 30% private use x (£588 x 20%). If the business use of the asset is 90% or more, any personal use is ignored, so you are not taxed on the provision of the asset.

6.3.5.　Even hiring a yacht

If the company hires the asset rather than buys it outright, and the hire charge is at least 20% of the cost of the asset, the cash equivalent value that you are taxed on is the cost the company incurs and not the smaller sum of 20% of the value of the asset.

Example

The company hires a boat for £1,200 to be used by you and your family for a month. The boat is valued at £30,000 at the time. So 20% of the value is £6,000, which is reduced to £500 (6,000 x 1/12), as the boat is only available for one month. However, because the hire cost of £1,200 is greater you are taxed on that sum instead.

KEY POINTS

- there's no employees' NI for you to pay on this benefit-in-kind
- computer equipment can be provided with no tax or NI charges arising provided certain conditions are met
- the company can deduct the cost of providing an asset to an employee from its profits, even if it's not used in the business
- instead of being taxed and NI'd on the full value of an asset if the company gave it to you, you only pay tax on 20% of the value each tax year
- if you keep the asset for more than five years, you will be taxed on more than it originally cost (five years x 20% p.a. = 100%)
- you are taxed on the cash equivalent value of the asset whether or not you actually use it during the year
- if you're taxed on the provision of the asset, the company will pay employers' NI on the cash equivalent value that appears on your P11D
- you will not own the asset the company provides, so you will not have the freedom to sell or change it if it's unsuitable.

CHAPTER 7

Loans to directors

7.1. INTRODUCTION

A loan from the company to a director can take many forms. It may be a formal arrangement under which the company provides you with funds which you agree to repay by a certain date, possibly with interest. Or it can be a payment in advance.

TAX BREAK

A loan is not classed as earnings, so it should not have tax or NI deducted under the PAYE system.

If the company puts down a deposit to help you buy a house or car, the money provided can either be treated as a bonus or a loan. If treated as a bonus, you will be taxed on the full amount paid by the company. However, if the deposit paid is treated as a loan to you by the company, you're not taxed on the amount of the advance, but you may be taxed on an official rate of interest (currently 4.75%) for the loan.

To take maximum advantage of this tax break you would need to take out a loan in excess of £5,000 (including any car or season ticket loan) from your company and be charged no interest on the outstanding balance. The Taxman would then calculate notional interest at 4.75% per annum on the outstanding balance during the tax year. This benefit-in-kind (BiK) is then taxed at your highest rate of tax.

Example

An interest-free bridging loan, if you are between house sales, of, say, £50,000 for six months would cost you £475 (£50,000 x 4.75% = £2,375 x 6/12 x 40%) in tax. What rate do mortgage companies charge for bridging finance? 4.75% must be cheaper.

If the loan is still outstanding nine months after your company's year-end, it has to pay over 25% of the balance to the Taxman. The company pays Class 1 A NI on the BiK, currently 12.8%.

As a source of inexpensive, short-term finance, a loan from your company is still relatively cheap, even though the interest rate is 4.75%.

7.2. HOW DO YOU SET ONE UP?

You can withdraw the loan in the form of a cheque, cash or transfer to your private bank account. However, the money paid needs to be accurately recorded as a loan in the company's accounts. The best way to do this is to have a separate account shown in the company's books as a director's loan account. This should record all the amounts paid to you as loans and the dates and values of any repayments you make.

You do not normally have to sign a loan agreement when you borrow money from your company. However, if you're not the only shareholder, company law states that you should get the written permission of the other shareholders before you can borrow more than £5,000.

You can withdraw money by cheque or cash payments, or the company may buy things for you and add the cost of these items to your director's account. If a close check is not kept on this account, you might draw more money out of the company than is due to you, so the account becomes overdrawn. This is treated as a loan while it's overdrawn.

7.2.1. What is the maximum loan you can have?

In principle, you can withdraw as much as you want as a loan. If you pay a reasonable level of interest to the company on the sum borrowed, you will not be taxed on the loan.

However, if you borrow more than £5,000 and pay only a very low rate of interest, or no interest at all, the Taxman says you have received a BiK of an interest-free loan, and will charge you tax on that benefit. The company may also have to pay a tax charge if the loan has not been repaid by nine months after the year in which you first received the loan.

7.3.   WHAT TO PUT ON YOUR TAX RETURN?

You do not have to show a company loan on your tax return. If you borrow less than £5,000, there are no tax consequences for you. Also, if the company is in the business of providing commercial loans and your loan is provided on similar commercial terms, you will not be taxed on it.

If you borrow more than £5,000 and pay less than the official interest rate (currently 4.75%) on the outstanding balance, you have received a BiK. The cash equivalent value of the benefit should be calculated by your employer and shown on Form P11D. The company must provide its directors with a copy of the information shown on their respective P11Ds by July 6 each year. You need to copy the details of taxable benefits onto the "Employment" pages of your tax return in the section titled "Benefits and expenses".

Warning. The loan is not taxable whilst it's still repayable to the company. If the loan is written off, or forgiven, so you do not have to pay it back, you will be taxed on the sum advanced as if it were a bonus.

7.4. HOW MUCH TAX WILL YOU PAY?

You do not have to pay tax on the loan from the company, but the cash equivalent value of the benefit of a low-interest loan will be taxed if the amount borrowed is more than £5,000. The rate of tax that applies to your earnings depends on your total taxable income during the tax year.

However, the loan must be repaid eventually, so you could end up taking a dividend or bonus to clear the loan, with their respective after-tax costs.

7.5. CHOICE OF INTEREST CALCULATION

If you take a beneficial (i.e. interest-free) loan of over £5,000 from your company, the Taxman expects it to calculate the official rate of interest on it. However, there are two methods of doing this which could provide a tax break for you.

The cash equivalent of a loan is the interest that would have been payable if the borrower had paid interest at the official rate, less any interest actually paid by the borrower.

Where loans exceed £5,000, there are two ways of calculating the taxable benefit: **(1)** the normal (averaging) method; and **(2)** the alternative (precise) method. The normal method is applied unless the taxpayer or the Taxman specifically elects to use the alternative method. Where the loan is not at the same level throughout the tax year, it can make a significant difference if one or other method is used.

Under the normal method you apply an average interest rate to an average loan balance. For example, if the loan was £8,000 on April 6 2009 but £5,000 on April 5 2010, the average (half the aggregate) is £6,500 ((£8,000 + £5,000)/2). The official rate was 4.75% for the whole of 2009/10 so this gives you a benefit figure of £309 (£6,500 x 4.75%).

If the loan was only outstanding for part of the year, then you have to multiply the average by M/12, where M is the number of whole months the loan was outstanding. A full month runs from the sixth of one month to the fifth of the next.

TAX BREAK

Where loans to directors exceed £5,000 but are repaid within the tax year, you include complete tax months only. A loan taken out on January 1 and repaid on March 31 is only outstanding for two months, not three. Repay a loan a couple of days before the fifth of the month. This results in the period from the previous month being ignored in the calculations.

Where the normal method uses a monthly basis, the precise method considers the amount of loan outstanding each day.

Disadvantage 1. Periods of less than a month can't be ignored as they can under the normal method.

Disadvantage 2. The average amount of loan outstanding can be higher on a daily basis. You can see why the Taxman likes it.

Where the alternative method of calculation will significantly increase the amount of benefit, the Taxman will insist on it being used. How will he know? The P11D only discloses the maximum balance in the year. However, the company accounts may make it clear that the loan was higher in the middle of the year than at the start or end. However, it's not always the case that the alternative is more expensive.

TIP

Make an annual appraisal of which method suits you, but only make an election yourself if you want to use the alternative method. An election lasts for one tax year only. You have 22 months from the end of the tax year in which to make an election, i.e. January 31.

TAX BREAK

Ask your company to calculate the interest using both the normal and precise method. Choose the one that means a lower taxable benefit for you. Under self-assessment you don't have to declare the higher benefit, so don't.

7.6.   LONGER TERM LOANS

A close company (not the director) has to pay an additional tax charge amounting to 25% of the loan, the so-called "Section 419 charge", if it makes a loan to one of its directors or shareholders and that loan is not repaid in full by nine months after the end of the accounting period during which the money was first provided. A close company is one that is controlled by its directors who are also the shareholders, or one that has five or fewer shareholders. The Section 419 tax charge is refunded by the Taxman nine months after the end of the accounting period in which the loan is repaid.

Example

The company makes a loan of £10,000 to a director on January 1 2010, which is reported in the company's Corporation Tax return for the year ended December 31 2010. The company pays a Section 419 tax charge of £2,500 (£10,000 x 25%) on October 1 2011 as the loan is still outstanding on that date. The loan is repaid in full to the company on November 30 2011 and this is reported in the company's return for the year ended December 31 2011. The Taxman repays the Section 419 tax charge by offsetting the £2,500 against Corporation Tax due for payment on October 1 2012.

TAX BREAK

Even if the loan remains outstanding for more than one accounting period, the Section 419 tax charge is only paid once.

Example

In the example above the loan is outstanding for the whole of the year 2010 and most of 2011, but the Section 419 tax charge is only levied once on October 1 2011. If the loan is not repaid until October 31 2013, there would be no further tax charged but the original Section 419 tax would not be refunded to the company until October 1 2014.

Warning. Any size of advance or loan can trigger a Section 419 charge. All loans are added together.

Technically, it's illegal for a company to lend more than £5,000 to one of its directors unless the shareholders have approved the loan and the money is to be used to help the individual perform their duties as a director of the company. If you want to borrow more than £5,000 from your company, you should tell all the shareholders how much you need, what the money is to be used for, and get their written approval. This procedure is to protect the funds the other shareholders have invested in the company from being siphoned off by one director. If you are the only shareholder and director of the company, this obviously does not apply.

Disclosure. Even if you are the only shareholder and director of the company, the annual accounts must show the value of loans outstanding to the director and their immediate family. This disclosure is required to inform the other people and organisations who are owed money by the company how their cash is being used. If a bank manager can see the funds lent to the company have been provided to the director for their own private purposes, they may not be very happy. The bank may have the power under its loan agreement to demand an immediate repayment, possibly from the director personally.

- you can borrow up to £5,000 from your company without being taxed personally. There's also no NI to pay on the loan while the capital borrowed is repayable

- if you borrow from your company at the beginning of its accounting year, the capital can remain outstanding for up to 21 months (the company year plus nine months) with no tax charge being applied to the company

- there are no formal loan approval procedures or application forms to complete when you borrow from your company

- you can pay either a very low rate of interest or no interest at all on a loan from your company. If you pay at least the official rate of interest of 4.75%, you can borrow without restriction at very favourable rates

- the loan capital must be repaid to the company at some point. If the loan is forgiven, you will be taxed on the capital sum as if you had received a bonus payment of that amount on the date the loan was forgiven

- if the loan is still outstanding nine months after the end of the accounting year during which it was provided, the company must pay a tax charge of 25% for the capital advanced, however big or small the amount of the loan. However, this is refundable after the loan has been cleared

- for a loan in excess of £5,000, you will be taxed on the cash value of the benefit of receiving a low-interest loan. Currently this is 4.75% of the loan balance, at your top rate of income tax

- the company must pay employers' NI on the cash equivalent value of the benefit of providing you with a low-interest loan

- if the loan is for more than £5,000, written approval should be obtained from all the company shareholders

- the company's annual accounts must disclose the nature and amounts of loans provided to the directors.

CHAPTER 8

Medical cover

8.1. INTRODUCTION

As a director, if your company pays for your medical treatment or contributes to an insurance scheme such as BUPA, there will be a taxable benefit. You are taxed on the costs incurred by your company, for example, a proportion of the total premium paid by the company. As a separate issue, it can also pay for periodic medical check-ups for both you and your family.

There is no taxable benefit, however, in providing:

- medical treatment outside the UK if the director is working abroad
- insurance for the cost of such treatment.

TAX BREAK

Include medical insurance as part of your remuneration package because it does not attract NI and the company can usually negotiate a lower premium than you as an individual would pay.

8.2. WHAT'S COVERED?

Private health insurance for medical treatment in the UK is taxable, whether you pay for the insurance and the company reimburses the cost, or the company pays for the insurance directly. However, the company may be able to negotiate a discount if it buys medical insurance for a number of its employees, directors and their families covered by one policy.

If you take out a medical insurance policy in your own name and the company pays the premiums for you, there will also be an NI cost, as the company has paid a liability on your behalf.

Other medical expenses may be only partially tax-free. For example, paying for a routine medical examination is tax-free but any treatments that result from it are taxable and will attract NI if paid for by the company. To avoid the company paying for treatments that involve an extra NI charge, it can arrange to pay for the medical examination directly and provide you with a voucher to redeem against the total medical bill.

If you need to use display screen equipment (DSE) for your work, the company can pay for a regular eye test and for any spectacles you need solely to use that DSE safely, completely tax-free. If only part of your requirement for glasses relates to DSE work, only that part will be tax-free if paid for by the company. It is important that you get an itemised receipt from the optician that details the cost of the eye test and the components of the spectacle cost if the company is to reimburse the expense.

Tax law does not limit how much can be spent on medical expenses.

8.3. WHAT TO PUT ON YOUR TAX RETURN?

You include the taxable value of the medical expenses on the "Employment" pages on your tax return.

The taxable value of medical expenses should be shown on the P11D the company prepares for you. It must provide you with a copy of the information included on Form P11D by July 6 after the end of the tax year. Of course, tax-free medical expenses (such as check-ups) do not have to be reported on your tax return.

8.4. AT WHAT RATE WILL MEDICAL EXPENSES FINALLY BE TAXED?

Taxable medical expenses are treated as if they were part of your salary, so the rate of tax will be the highest that applies to your salary.

8.5. WHEN WILL YOU BE TAXED ON MEDICAL EXPENSES?

When the medical expenses are taxable, their value should be reported on Form P11D each tax year.

If the company pays the same amount of taxable medical expenses on your behalf each year, the Taxman will include that amount in your tax code. The operation of that code will allow (approximately) the right amount of tax to be deducted from your monthly salary.

KEY POINTS

- you can achieve a cost saving by the company paying for medical insurance on a group basis

- the company can pay for routine health checks for you and your family completely free of tax and NI

- if you need to use DSE as part of your job, the company can pay for a regular eye test and the cost of the prescription that relates to using the DSE. You don't have to pay tax or NI on these costs

- when you are required to work overseas the company can pay for medical insurance and any medical treatment you need with no tax or NI charges arising

- the cost of medical treatment (other than when working abroad), and insurance for that treatment is taxable and subject to an employers' NI charge

- the prescription for your spectacle lenses must relate to your work using DSE. The tax exemption will not cover the cost of the glasses you need, e.g., for driving or other distance viewing.

CHAPTER 9

<u>Childcare</u>

9.1. INTRODUCTION

Paying for childcare can use up a large proportion of your salary, so if your company can bear that cost, you will be better off. There are two tax-efficient ways for the company to do this:

1. **Childcare vouchers.** A childcare voucher has a face value of a certain monetary amount which can be redeemed against the cost of places for children under 16, in approved nurseries or with registered childminders who participate in the voucher scheme.

2. **Workplace nursery.** A workplace nursery is the provision of supervised childcare on premises made available by the company. Such provision is tax and NI-free.

> **TAX BREAK**
>
> Childcare vouchers up to £55 per week are free of employees' NI and childcare provided through a workplace nursery is free of income tax and NI.

> **TAX BREAK**
>
> The £55 limit is per parent rather than per child. So if your spouse works in the company as well, you can extract £110 per week tax-free.

News. In a U-turn decision, the government has announced that tax relief on childcare vouchers will continue after April 2011. This is a reversal of previous proposals to scrap tax and NI contribution exemptions for childcare vouchers provided by employers. However, from April 2011 the tax relief will be applied for all at the basic rate of 20%, regardless of what rate you pay tax.

> **TIP**
>
> Sign up for a childcare scheme before April 2011 in order to be able to benefit from NI savings from it until at least 2015.

Warning. If you currently receive tax credits, then you may be worse off by taking vouchers than, say, increased salary.

9.2. HOW DO YOU SET THIS UP?

9.2.1. Childcare vouchers

The vouchers are usually provided by specialist agencies that charge a handling or administration fee of up to 8% of the face value of the voucher. If you buy the childcare voucher personally and the company then reimburses the cost, both you and the company must pay NI on this amount. The childcare vouchers must not be exchangeable for cash. If they are, NI is again payable.

9.2.2. Workplace nursery

This can be either in the same building that the company occupies or in another building hired or acquired for the purpose. The requirements of a workplace nursery may also be met if the company helps to run a commercial nursery. Where the company merely pays for places in a commercial nursery, the childcare provision will not count as a workplace nursery, and it will be taxable.

9.3. ANY UPPER LIMIT?

Childcare vouchers. There is no upper limit on the value of childcare vouchers you can provide.

Workplace nursery. The company can only provide tax-free childcare for the children who normally live with you, or your own children that you maintain financially. The company cannot provide free childcare for, e.g., your grandchildren or nieces and nephews, unless you are financially responsible for them.

9.4. WHAT TO PUT ON YOUR TAX RETURN?

Childcare vouchers in excess of £55 per week are a taxable benefit so their cost should be reported on your tax return.

The cash equivalent value of the voucher must be included on the "Employment" pages of your tax return under the heading "Benefits and expenses". The figure is the full cost of the voucher to the company, which is the face value of the voucher plus any administration or handling fee paid by the company. The company should report this figure on your P11D, and provide you with the relevant details by July 6 each year.

A workplace nursery is tax-free, as long as it meets the strict legal requirements. So you're not required to report the provision of these childcare places on your tax return.

9.5.   AT WHAT RATE WILL YOU BE TAXED?

Childcare vouchers in excess of the £55 tax and NI-free limit are taxable as part of your total income, so the rate of tax applied to the cash equivalent value will be the highest rate that applies to your income in a tax year.

The provision of childcare through a workplace nursery is tax-free.

The Taxman should adjust your tax coding to take account of the value of the vouchers received in the previous year. So if you receive the same value of vouchers each year, the income tax due should be deducted in advance through the PAYE system.

KEY POINTS

- childcare vouchers can save you many thousands of pounds a year in childminder fees
- your company can provide tax-free childcare for your children and those of your employees by setting up a workplace nursery
- the first £55 per week of childcare vouchers is free of both employees' and employers' NI and income tax when they are purchased directly by the company
- vouchers are not completely tax-free. The cost of childcare vouchers in excess of £55 is taxable in the hands of the recipients
- if the company reimburses you for the cost of childcare, or for childcare vouchers you have purchased, those costs are taxable and subject to NI.

CHAPTER 10

Expenses

10.1. INTRODUCTION

Most directors will want their company to meet the cost of all expenses which could be said to have a business connection or relationship, no matter how remote that connection might be.

Although a director can claim tax relief under the general rule for those expenses that are "wholly, exclusively and necessarily incurred in the performance of the duties of employment", this is notoriously restrictive terminology. From a tax break point of view it's generally sensible to arrange that the company meets all expenses (directly or by reimbursement) which would not have been incurred but for the existence of the directorship.

In an ideal scenario you would charge every penny you spend against the business and pay no taxes at all, but that is unrealistic. After all, if your company were consistently showing losses but you continued to live a privileged lifestyle, the Taxman would start making a few enquiries.

The reality is that the line between private and business lives can get blurred and you can't always tell where one ends and the other begins. For example, how many people take work home with them? If the accounts are done on the dining room table, is the cost of heating and lighting that room attributable to business or private use? What about telephone calls or using the Internet for research? How many people pick up bits and pieces for the office along with groceries? Does that make it a business trip? And the newspaper you read every morning with the business section…?

The list could go on, but the point is clear: there are times as a director when what you previously thought of as private expenses will now have a work-related element to them. These can in whole, or in part, be quite legitimately charged against your company's profit.

We are not advocating taking liberties with the tax rules. There are clear principles that have to be followed for the expense claim to be considered legitimate by the Taxman.

10.2. DISPENSATIONS FOR DIRECTORS' EXPENSES

TAX BREAK

A dispensation is an agreement with the Taxman that certain expense payments made do not need to be included on the P11D or on the tax return, the only proviso being that they attract a full tax deduction in the hands of the employee.

In a nutshell, the amount being refunded to the employee exactly covers the amount you would have been able to claim back on your tax return and therefore the Taxman isn't going to be out of pocket.

10.2.1. What can be covered?

The Taxman's website says any type of expenses payment (apart from round sum allowances) and most benefits-in-kind can be covered, including:

- qualifying travel expenses
- entertaining
- subscriptions to professional bodies
- non-cash vouchers and credit tokens to cover expenses.

The Taxman will only allow a dispensation if he is sure that:

- no tax would be payable by the employee on expenses paid
- expenses claims are independently checked and authorised within the firm and, where, possible, are supported by receipts.

The second condition presents a problem where the owner-manager of the business is the sole employee, or if the directors are effectively authorising their own expense claims.

> **TIP**
>
> It's still possible to use the system if the expenses claimed are fully supported by documentation and the company's accountant regularly reviews a sample of them.

10.3. CLAIMING IT'S PART OF YOUR REMUNERATION

Let's say you've incurred some expenses partly for business and partly for personal reasons. The rule is that expenses must be wholly and exclusively incurred for the purpose of the business. This leads to the most important principle, which is duality of purpose, which means if you incur some expenses only partly for business reasons, you don't get part of your expenses allowed - you will get none of them.

Tax break

In order to manage the business, a company has to attract and retain key employees. The cost of this normally meets the wholly and exclusively test, provided it's not excessive for the duties performed. Therefore, if, as a director, you reassess your remuneration package to include a particular expense you would like the company to incur (as a benefit-in-kind for yourself) this is, in our opinion, wholly and exclusively for the purposes of the trade.

Remember, directors' remuneration is determined by the shareholders of the company. However, if challenged on this part of your remuneration argument by the Taxman, you'll need to be able to provide him with a copy of what was agreed in writing between you and your company - both your board minutes and the addition to your contract of employment.

The board minute could include a commercial reason for the company agreeing to add this expense to your remuneration package with the company.

Example 1. Board minute

In recognition of your contribution to the Company and to avoid you spending time away from the company business at key times to undertake DIY, the company has decided that as part of your remuneration package it will contract and pay for the painting and decorating of two rooms in your principal private residence each year. This is, of course, subject to the company having sufficient funds to do so.

Example 2. Amendment to contract of employment

As from April 10 2010 the company will contract and pay for the painting and decorating of two rooms in your principle private residence each year. This benefit-in-kind is from that date part of your remuneration package and will be provided subject to the Company having sufficient funds to do so.

Tip

If you have gone to the trouble of getting the company's paperwork right, so that an expense can legitimately be treated as a benefit-in-kind, make sure it appears on your P11D. Otherwise, the Taxman might argue that it's earnings and tax it more heavily.

10.3.1. What sort of expenses?

Some things to include in your contract of employment you might not have thought of are:

- garden maintenance
- paying for your holiday
- school fees
- private tutors
- language lessons
- company plane (or yacht)
- tax advisor's fees.

10.4. BOARD MINUTES GENERALLY

Some time in the future the Taxman may enquire into your company's expenses. If so, he likes to put his own spin on your innocent actions by saying your decision was made for the "purpose of avoiding tax". But there is something you can do now with your company's board minutes that will later stop him in his tracks.

The Taxman has no right to tell you how to run your business. He can apply tax law but he will have trouble making it stick in borderline areas if you can show the expenditure was intended to benefit the business.

Generally, any note of, for example, a telephone call or a meeting, made at the time or shortly afterwards can be produced as evidence in a dispute as it shows your intentions were good.

The directors of the company may have to consult each other, albeit informally. But some of these meetings have to be on a formal basis so that decisions taken are recorded as board minutes - which then form a statutory record.

Most company minute books are on a shelf somewhere gathering dust. All they usually contain are a few pages of meetings, share allotments and directors' appointments. But they can be used to record other matters such as the leasing or purchase of premises and agreement to loans and bank overdrafts. In practice, these things are considered before the meeting and are only put to the board for approval. So all that gets recorded is the decision. But it can be used to set up your tax breaks.

> **TIP**
>
> Record your good intentions in a board minute at the time you make your decision. In cases where you think there might be a problem, post the signed minutes to the board members' home addresses. Keep yours and the envelope it came in to prove it was done on time.

To charge penalties the Taxman has to show that you were careless etc. in your tax affairs. A timely minute can make that charge difficult to sustain. If, down the line, the Taxman wants to put another spin on things, you've put up a stop sign. This way you stay one step ahead of him.

10.5. ADVANCES FOR EXPENSES

In the Taxman's view a loan means more than just lending money, it includes any form of credit. It follows for him that *"any kind of advance by reason of employment is a loan. For example any amount shown in the employer's books or records as owed by a director or employee will count as a loan."*

As long as the total amount outstanding on all loans from the employer to the director does not exceed £5,000 at any time in the tax year, then they are ignored for the purpose of the rules on beneficial loans.

This is an all or nothing exemption. If, however briefly, the loan balance rises above £5,000 in the tax year, the exemption is not available. A director with a loan of £5,000 who is also given an advance for expenses of £1,000 will have a tax liability because the total loan balance of £6,000 exceeded the £5,000 tax-free exemption. Employers' NI will also be due on what is now a taxable benefit-in-kind.

Loans to directors over £5,000 are prohibited under the Companies Act unless they are disclosed both in the company's accounts and in the annual return of benefits and expenses (P11D). However, there is a get-out clause.

10.5.1. Up to £1,000

An advance on account of expenses to be incurred by an employee is strictly a loan for tax purposes. However, the Taxman has a statement of practice which removes certain advances from the net. The main conditions that need to be satisfied are: **(1)** maximum amount advanced at any one time must not exceed £1,000; **(2)** advances must be spent within six months; and **(3)** the employee must account for how they have spent the amount advanced.

The common sense interpretation of an "advance" that takes you over the £5,000 loan limit will not have a tax liability. However, it would be worth obtaining the Taxman's agreement (in writing) to this before the "advance" is granted.

If an amount advanced is subsequently written off, rather than used for business expenditure, then there will be a tax charge on that write-off.

10.5.2. Over £1,000

On those (rare) occasions where you might need an advance of more than £1,000 for expenses, what happens then? Such amounts need to be reported on Form P11D. However, as long as there is a reasonable justification for having exceeded the £1,000 limit, e.g. a lengthy overseas business trip, then the Taxman will not, in practice, treat the advance as a loan.

The concession only applies to the advance on account of expenses. Expenses payments themselves must be included on the Form P11D in the usual way. Of course, any advances that do not meet the conditions would need to be included on the P11D for that employee anyway.

TAX BREAK

Exceeding the tax-free limit of £5,000 for small loans results in a tax liability. However, if you keep an advance to less than £1,000 and it's spent within six months it won't be treated as a loan. So problem solved.

KEY POINTS

- a director can claim tax relief under the general rule for those expenses that are wholly, exclusively and necessarily incurred in the performance of their duties of employment
- from a tax break point of view it's generally sensible to arrange that the company meets all business expenses (directly or by reimbursement)
- your company should be able to get an agreement (a dispensation) with the Taxman that certain expense payments made do not need to be included on the P11D or your tax return. The amount being refunded to the director must exactly match the amount they would have been able to claim back on their tax return
- where the owner-manager of the business is the sole employee, or if the directors are effectively authorising their own expense claims, it's still possible to use the dispensation system if the expenses claimed are fully supported by documentation and the company's accountant regularly reviews a sample of them
- an advance on account of expenses to be incurred by a director is strictly a loan for tax purposes. However, advances up to a £1,000 which meet certain conditions can be ignored.

CHAPTER 11

Working from home

11.1. INTRODUCTION

If you work at home on a regular basis, what can you claim for? As an employee, you can claim expenses for the costs you incur by doing so. Your employer needs to agree that you will undertake some of your work at home on a regular basis, under a homeworking arrangement.

The extra household costs you can claim include the increased energy needed to heat and light the property for longer and the extra water used, if that's metered. However, you can't claim a proportion of your mortgage or Council Tax payments, as these amounts are fixed whether or not you work from home.

When you work at home regularly, but not full-time, your claim for expenses must be made to your employer, not directly to the Taxman. The claim must also be supported by receipts, showing the increased energy, water etc. used due to you working at home.

11.2. £3 A WEEK TAX-FREE

Instead of collecting together household bills you can claim a tax-free rate of up to £3 a week from your employer, with no questions asked by the Taxman. No receipts are required for expenses being paid for, and your employer can still pay for, e.g., the cost of business telephone calls, in addition to the weekly rate.

TAX BREAK

If your working at home costs are less than £3 per week, or are too difficult to measure, just ask your employer if they will pay the tax-free rate of £3 per week: £156 per year. However, they can reimburse you for the actual extra energy bills and other costs incurred by working from home if these amount to more than £3 per week.

11.3. CHARGING RENT

What's the best way of charging your company for use of your office at home? And if you work for several companies, can you bill each of them?

TAX BREAK

Record any payment to you by your company for use of your home as rent (including services such as access and use of an Internet connection), both in your company's books as an expense and on your own tax return as income. However, on your tax return you now get to claim for any additional costs of meeting your company's homeworking or storage requirements for, say, stock in your garage.

Your company will get a tax deduction for the rent paid (provided it's not excessive). And if the rental income is matched by your expenses, you will have a zero tax bill. Plus, you avoid arguing with the Taxman whether these expenses are wholly, exclusively and necessarily for the furtherance of your job. If sold, you would not pay any Capital Gains Tax on the home office part of your house if it were a common area. So use it for private as well as business purposes.

11.3.1. Paperwork

Back this up with a licence agreement between you and your company setting out the terms and conditions. Include the additional measures/services your company expects you to take/provide.

11.3.2. More than one company

Yes, you could charge several companies. However, you only have costs to cover/ match the income from one. You would have to declare the income from the others on your tax return and be taxed on this rental income/profit. However, one solution, if there are three companies, would be to charge them a third each or load it towards the one you do most work for at home.

> **TIP**
>
> One company could use your house whilst another could use your garage (see 11.6.). On your tax return you now get to claim for any additional costs of meeting a company's requirements for the safe keeping of its stock/records whilst in your garage, providing that's not where you keep your car of course!

11.4. CLAIMING THE COST OF YOUR BROADBAND

If your company reimburses you the cost of your broadband connection (at home), you could end up with a tax bill. However, there's another way to structure this to avoid the problem. What's involved? In many businesses, there's a clear need for directors to create, submit or receive and comment on work whilst at home. For example, the last minute agenda for the board meeting together with all the documents that are going to be discussed. But what are the tax consequences of the company paying for a broadband Internet connection to facilitate this?

A simple administrative approach would be to pay a cash allowance towards your Internet costs related to work. It's then left to you to claim a tax deduction on your tax return for the actual cost of business calls. Both income tax and NI (employees' and employers') is payable on the rental, plus private calls.

TIP

For any amount over £3 per week, get your company to put the whole allowance through the payroll as a taxable addition to salary. Otherwise you might end up with a surprise tax bill later.

The alternative is to have any bill (from the service provider) in the name of the employer, not you. The advantage of this is that your company doesn't have to put it through the payroll as it's classed as a benefit-in-kind.

Example

You're taxable on the monthly broadband connection charge (including VAT). Yes, there's no employees' NI, but your company has to pay employers' NI on this benefit-in-kind. For example, if the monthly charge is £25 (including VAT) that's a benefit-in-kind value of £300 per annum on which employers' NI of £38.40 will be due. Your tax bill will be £60 (£300 x 20%), £120 (£300 x 40%) or £150 (£300 x 50%) depending on the rate of tax you pay, which is significantly cheaper than paying out £300 a year for broadband personally. However, you do have to pay some income tax.

Some providers will not allow a company-billed connection at a domestic address, so you would need to reclaim the expense from the company.

TAX BREAK

Charge your company rent for its use of your "home office", remembering to include services in this rental charge. In this case, include a figure for access and use of a broadband Internet connection. Put the rent on your tax return but offset by expenses, including the cost of broadband.

TIP

For a test period (including weekends) work out the business use of the broadband connection. Keep your own log of how much time you spend privately online. Use this as a basis for saying, for example, that 90% of the broadband usage is work-related. So your company should pay (as part of their rent) for 90% of the annual connection cost.

Working from home

11.5. BUSINESS RATES?

You work from home but are concerned that you might be building up a business rates liability. As a good citizen you might be tempted to ask your local authority whether business rates would become payable if your company were to pay you a fixed amount of rent of, say, £150 per month. If you did this your query would be passed to the Valuation Office who would probably have to "send someone round" to inspect the room you wish to rent out to the business. As a rough estimate, business rates could cost as much as £500 a year!

The Valuation Office has a factsheet on working from home. It says, *"The part of the property used for work may be liable to business rates"*. "May" not "will", which is good news. From the examples given in the factsheet, business rates apply to a room that is used exclusively for business. Where it has mostly domestic use, then normal Council Tax applies. It's obviously a matter of degree and how much the room has been adapted for non-domestic use.

TIP

Saying "rent" will be paid implies an exclusive right to occupy. The company should have a licence to use the premises, for say, 35 hours per week, plus a fee for storage of papers. It all comes down to the terms of the agreement with the property owner (you), which any solicitor could argue more fully if the Taxman bothered to dispute it.

TAX BREAK

If you *charge your company rent* for the provision of an office in your home, there's no need to contact your local authority and ask to pay business rates. Keep quiet and the rates department won't bother you. Make sure the rent is paid under a licence that doesn't give your company exclusive use, e.g. it's only available to them between 9am and 5pm and there's a TV or an exercise bike in the room as well.

11.6. USING YOUR OWN GARAGE

If you had to store, say, product samples for your customers in your own garage, is it possible to claim some storage costs in addition to those claimed for using your home as an office?

You should easily be able to come up with additional costs incurred wholly, exclusively and necessarily by using your garage for storage. Here are eight to get you started:

1. Some products must not be exposed to high or low temperatures, so a proportion of household electricity costs to cover use of a heater in winter or a fan in summer should be claimed.

2. Any storage boxes/cages.

3. Additional insurance premiums.

4. Security measures - from a more secure door, through to sensor-activated lights to an alarm system.

5. Additional lighting.

6. Weather proofing.

7. Smoke alarm, fire extinguisher, sand bucket (particularly for chemical spills) etc.

8. The cost of a trolley to move products to and from the car/van - health and safety must be observed at all times.

Any allowance paid by your employer to you for the use of your garage counts as earnings. Therefore, PAYE should be applied to the payment. This will be the case whether or not the garage is attached to your home.

TAX BREAK

Where an employer claims that the payment to an employee is rent chargeable on the employee as property income, then this is tax-deductible for the company and not earnings of the employee. So any payment to you by your employer for use of your garage should be recorded as rent, both in your company's books as an expense, and on your own tax return as income. However, on your return you now get to claim for any additional costs of meeting your company's requirements for the safe-keeping etc. of that stock whilst in your garage.

TIP

Back up the rental claim with a formal licence agreement between you and your employer setting out the terms and conditions of this rental agreement. Include the additional measures your company expects you to take over preserving the condition of the stock.

KEY POINTS

- if your working at home costs are less than £3 per week, or are too difficult to measure, just ask your employer if they will pay the tax-free rate of £3 per week: £156 per year. However, they can reimburse you for the actual extra energy bills and other costs if these amount to more than £3 per week

- the most tax efficient way is to record any payment to you by your company as rent. It could be for using your garage as well as a room in your house

- you shouldn't be paying business rates if your company does not have exclusive use of the facilities. Restrict business use from, e.g. 9am to 5pm.

CHAPTER 12

Pension contributions

12.1. INTRODUCTION

Pension funds have always enjoyed many tax benefits, including the ability to receive investment income and enjoy capital growth in a tax-free environment. However, a new regime for private pension provision started on April 6 2006, commonly referred to as "A Day". In broad terms, from A Day beneficial tax treatment is given provided your overall amount invested within a pension fund remains within two separate allowances: **(1)** the annual contribution allowance; and **(2)** the lifetime allowance.

Annual contribution. This is set at £255,000 for 2010/11. If you exceed this, you will be taxed personally on the excess at 40%.

Lifetime limit. There's also a limit of £1.8 million on the pension value attracting relief for 2010, to be reviewed at five-yearly intervals after that. Any excess is subject to a recovery charge when you draw benefits from the fund. You will pay tax at 25% on the excess funds used to create a pension and 40% on those taken as a lump sum.

TAX BREAK

Tax relief for contributions to a registered pension scheme are generous in that income tax relief is given on the greater of £3,600 (gross or 100% of your taxable earnings). Your taxable earnings broadly include employment income and benefits - dividends and investment income are not included.

Although tax relief is limited to the annual allowance, there is no pension earnings cap. This gives considerably more flexibility for you as a high earner.

12.2. COMPANY CONTRIBUTIONS

Before A Day, the maximum contribution a company could make on behalf of one of its directors was based on a percentage of their salary. So if you only received a nominal salary with the balance of the remuneration taken in the form of dividends, the amount that could be paid into your pension scheme (by either you or the company) was restricted to £3,600 a year.

There's no longer any limit on the maximum contribution your company can make. However, in practice, it's likely that the company contributions will still be restricted so that they do not exceed the "annual allowance" (£255,000 for 2010/11) because you will be liable to a 40% tax charge on any contributions in excess of this figure.

A separate but important issue is whether your company will be able to get full tax relief for such sizeable pension contributions.

Although the company can pay an unlimited contribution into your pension, it only gets a tax deduction if the contribution passes the "wholly and exclusively" for the business test.

How will the Taxman apply this "wholly and exclusively" test? In practice, HMRC looks to see whether or not the contributions paid in respect of a director are in line with that which would have been made to fund the pension provision of an unconnected employee in a similar situation. In other words, it's likely that HMRC may try to restrict tax relief where substantial contributions are paid in respect of a controlling director or their family.

TAX BREAK

Get the company to make a large payment into your pension scheme as a bonus only in years that it reaches a certain level of profit. This then gives commercial justification for the payment.

Your company's contribution to your pension scheme can be deducted as a trading expense in the period it is paid up to the annual allowance figure (currently £255,000 per year regardless of your earnings). Any amount the company pays in excess of this is taxed on you.

However, in practice you should be able to claim relief for substantial pension contributions (up to the annual allowance) given that directors invariably carry on considerably more onerous and responsible work than ordinary employees.

The Taxman has relaxed his stance somewhat with the following guide to his inspectors: *"Controlling directors are often the driving force behind the company. Where the controlling director is also the person whose work generates the company's income, then the level of the remuneration package is a commercial decision and it is unlikely that there will be a non-business purpose for the level of the remuneration package. It should be noted that remuneration does not include entitlement to dividends etc. arising in the capacity of shareholder."*

"Where the remuneration package paid in respect of other directors is in line with that paid to unconnected employees, you should accept that the package is paid wholly and exclusively for the purposes of the trade."

TIP

A large pension contribution is particularly attractive if you are over 55 years old, since you can draw funds from your pension scheme (without retiring), taking a tax-free lump sum equivalent to 25% of the fund, and income can be drawn from the fund without NI due.

12.3. CHANGE FOR HIGH EARNERS

The "special annual allowance" pension relief legislation is so complex it's difficult to follow it. Basically, subject to certain exceptions, anyone making a one-off or irregular pension contribution with a relevant income (RI) exceeding £130,000 per year will have their tax relief capped at £20,000 in any one tax year.

However, you can still get higher rate tax relief on pension premiums paid in excess of £20,000 if you pay them quarterly, or more often, and this arrangement existed before last year's Budget on April 22 2009.

The problems only start when your RI is greater than £130,000. So one solution is to reduce earnings to below that amount. Even if it's only by £1 it's sufficient to stop the restriction of tax relief being triggered.

You could cut your salary to reduce your RI below £130,000 and get your **company** to pay some or all of this into a pension fund. But this triggers special anti-avoidance rules. The Taxman ignores the salary sacrifice you've made so that your RI isn't treated as reduced. But you can get around this.

Loophole 1 - the "unconnected" rule. There's a loophole that means the salary sacrifice rules don't apply if the income you give up isn't linked to the extra money the **company** pays into your pension fund. If you sacrifice earnings but several months later increase them, your **company** could pay that increase into a pension fund for you without triggering the anti-avoidance rules. The key is justifying the increase, e.g. because of higher profits or more hours worked.

Loophole 2 - employers' contributions. The Taxman has carefully worded his advice on the salary sacrifice rules. What he doesn't tell you is that the rules only apply where the salary sacrificed is paid into a pension on your behalf. It doesn't affect premiums you pay personally.

T**IP**

Make use of this loophole and get your RI below £130,000 by exchanging salary for a benefit-in-kind worth as much to you but which has a lower value for tax purposes.

Example

Suppose your RI for pension purposes is £160,000 and you pay a one-off pension premium of £40,000, the tax relief will be subject to the £20,000 cap. But if you sacrifice salary of £15,000 in exchange for a company car of equal value (with CO_2 emissions of 164g/km), your RI would drop to £148,000 (£145,000 + £3,000 annual benefit-in-kind charge). You could get full tax relief on the whole premium. So, with no real cost to you you've gained tax relief of £4,000, i.e. an extra 20% of £20,000.

Pension contributions

Don't just think company cars, consider childcare vouchers, low or interest-free loans, bicycles etc. All of these can be substituted for an equal value salary sacrifice to reduce your RI.

TAX BREAK

Cut income to below £130,000 to avoid restrictions on pension relief. Do this by cutting salary and replacing it with a *company* pension contribution. Justify this as a reward for, say, working more hours. Tax relief on premiums won't be restricted if you lower your income to below £130,000 by exchanging salary for benefits with a lower tax value.

KEY POINTS

- substantial company pension contributions in respect of directors must be capable of justification (based on the entire reward package, including the contribution)
- consider a company pension (self-administered) scheme for directors to be used as a tax-saving vehicle
- you can hold up to £1.8m (2010/11) in a pension fund on a tax-privileged basis
- there is much greater flexibility on the drawing of pension benefits since A Day (April 6 2006)
- you have the ability to draw your pension benefits whilst continuing to work in your company
- consider the use of salary sacrifice arrangements as a means of securing higher company pension contributions.

CHAPTER 13

Share schemes

13.1. INTRODUCTION

Offering employees shares in a business is an increasingly popular part of pay packages - particularly for businesses whose shares are traded on the Stock Exchange.

Offering shares is a more complicated kind of reward than paying employees cash. However, it can be much more effective in linking the **objectives** of the business, e.g. profit maximisation, and the objectives of employees, e.g. make a large gain on the value of shares held.

Many employers do give directors and employees the opportunity to acquire shares in their companies at advantageous terms. Their aim is to provide a performance incentive and is often a form of "golden handcuff".

13.1.1. Free or cheap shares

However, HMRC is keen to ensure that when a director/employee receives free or cheap shares, either from a direct share award or the exercise of a share option, any profit or reward element in shares/share options is taxed as employment income, i.e. the shares have been received by reason of employment. The tax charge is based on the benefit received, which is broadly calculated by reference to the market value of the shares less any consideration paid by the employee.

The gift of shares in recognition of a director's performance (or even long service) will generally be taxable in the director's hands as employment income. Since there's no market for most shares in private companies, the director will need to declare this income under self-assessment, not PAYE. There should, however, be no NI on the gift.

The income tax liability will be based on the value of the shares. A minority holding in a private company will usually be heavily discounted and is not simply a fraction of the price of the company. The value will need to be agreed with HMRC. The company's accountants may be able to do this, or it may be necessary to employ a specialist valuer.

The company can meet any tax liability on behalf of the employee; however, this will give rise to PAYE and NI obligations on the amount of tax.

13.2. SHARE OPTIONS

An alternative to "free or cheap shares" for a company could be to give the director the right to acquire options over shares in the company. There are several tax-efficient share schemes which generally have the advantage of there being no up-front tax. The most commonly adopted of these are Enterprise Management Incentives. These are relatively cheap to implement and, of particular interest, the company can impose requirements to limit which employees are able to benefit. In order for the company to qualify they must meet requirements as to the trade and the size and ownership of the company.

Tax break

If one of the tax effective schemes is used, when the shares are sold often there will be no income tax or NI on the grant or exercise of the options. When the shares are sold there will be a Capital Gains Tax (CGT) charge on the employees based on any uplift in value between the price paid and the price achieved on sale. Capital gains are currently taxed at 18% as opposed to 20%-50% for income, so there's a clear attraction for employees. With no tax upfront, share options are often preferable to more straightforward gifts of shares.

In the past it was possible to minimise income tax charges on employee shares by making the acquisition conditional or by restricting their rights in some way, thus depressing the value that would be subject to income tax. However, there is now a general anti-avoidance provision which negates any tax savings along these lines.

Share schemes which are approved by HMRC offer tax and NI breaks not available to unapproved schemes.

Example

Diane is granted an option over 10,000 shares in her employer's company. To exercise these options she must pay £2 a share. Five years later, the shares in question are worth £5 per share. Diane exercises her option, pays £20,000 and is issued with £10,000 shares. Her gain is £30,000; the value of shares at exercise £50,000 (£5 x £10,000) less price paid £20,000 (£2 x £10,000). Diane's income tax bill on £30,000 as a 40% rate taxpayer would be £12,000.

If this had been an HMRC approved scheme, Diane's profit would have been subject to CGT not income tax. Therefore, her tax bill would only have been £3,582 (gain of £30,000 less £10,100 annual exemption = £19,900 x 18%). A saving of £8,418 (£12,000 - £3,582).

Tip

If the size of the gain which a director realises is relatively small and they typically make no capital gains, the opportunity to utilise the annual exemption is likely to be significant and could lead to an effective rate of tax which is considerably below the 18% headline CGT rate.

13.3. THE DIFFERENT SCHEMES

The way to bring an option profit within the 18% CGT regime is to use one of HMRC's approved share option schemes, such as a company share option plan, or the tax favoured Enterprise Management Incentives. If all employees are to have options, then a save-as-you-earn scheme can be used. Provided the conditions of the schemes are complied with (and if required HMRC approval obtained), there is generally no income tax or NI charge on either the grant or exercise of the option.

On the subsequent sale of the shares any gain is subject to CGT as for unapproved schemes, although the base cost for CGT will be the exercise price of the shares and not the market value at the date of exercise. Entrepreneurs' relief may be available to reduce the effective rate of tax on disposal.

Conditions which have to be met to meet HMRC's approval include that:

- the exercise price must not differ significantly from the market value of the shares when the option is granted

- the value of the shares under option which can be held by any one employee is limited to £30,000 (measured at the date of grant)

- options can't be exercised tax-free less than three years or more than ten years after the grant of an option (but this rule is relaxed for "good" leavers).

Options can't be granted to employees who hold more than 25% (10% before July 10 2003) of the shares in the company, but they can be offered to selected employees.

There are various schemes available which companies can use to offer shares as part of the remuneration package.

13.3.1. Employee share ownership plans (ESOPs)

ESOPs involve setting up a trust into which a company offers shares in the business. In the UK a company using an ESOP can give employees shares worth up to £3,000 each year. The gains made on these shares are free of tax (CGT) as long as they are held in trust for more than five years.

13.3.2. Share option schemes

These are a popular way of incentivising senior management and key employees. Under a share option scheme, selected employees are given the right to buy shares at their current price, at a later date. If the shares increase in value in the meantime, employees will make an immediate profit when they *"exercise"* their options.

In the UK, employees may hold options on shares worth up to £30,000. The option can be exercised after three years but not later than ten years. Again, there is no tax paid on any gains made by exercising these options.

13.3.3. Sharesave schemes

Sharesave schemes are made available to all employees - who must be able to participate in the scheme on equal terms. All scheme members get the right - but not the obligation - to buy a number of shares (normally lower than their current price) after three, five or seven years.

In the meantime, employee members save a regular amount to pay for the shares. If the shares rise in value, employees have a profit when they buy the shares. No income tax is paid on any gains made on these shares.

When a company is incorporated, the directors will be asked to give details of how many shares the company has and who owns them. In the case of small businesses - there may only be two shares, one given to each director. This gives each of them an equal stake in the business and prevents one or other from making hasty decisions about the running of the business without consulting the other.

As companies become larger and more financially viable they can pursue the option of providing additional shares. These shares are - if the company is not floated on the stock market - offered as incentives or investment opportunities to the staff, family of staff members or the general public.

13.3.4. Approved company share option plans (CSOP)

The approved CSOP is a flexible tax-advantaged share option scheme. The scheme does not have to be open to all employees, so in general, companies have used this scheme to reward directors and senior employees.

KEY POINTS

- no income tax or NI is charged on the grant of an option
- no income tax or NI is charged on the exercise of the option or on any increase in the value of the shares between the date the option was granted and the date it was exercised, provided the exercise date is more than three years after the grant
- any gain on the eventual disposal of the shares is subject to Capital Gains Tax, benefiting from the 18% tax rate and the annual exemption (currently £10,100). The base cost of the shares is the amount paid for them under the option plus the amount paid for the option
- the costs of setting up the scheme are tax deductible for your company.

PART 2

Director/shareholder

CHAPTER 14

Dividends

14.1. INTRODUCTION

Becoming a shareholder in your company as well as a director is good news from a tax break point of view because you can now receive dividends on those shares. The key advantage is that whilst salaries and bonuses attract NI contributions, dividends do not. There is even no income tax to pay on a certain level of dividend. However, excessive dividends can push you into higher rates of income tax. The most tax-efficient solution will always depend on your particular circumstances but could involve diverting this higher rate dividend to other members of your family.

For your company's point of view, if it pays Corporation Tax (CT) at 21% or less, it's more tax-efficient for it to pay profits out as a dividend rather than as a bonus. However, with CT at the top rate of 28%, it will pay more tax overall by retaining profits to pay out as a dividend rather than distributing a similar amount as, say, a bonus. Generally, therefore, a dividend is good news all round from a tax saving point of view.

14.2. THE TAX BREAK DIVIDEND

TAX BREAK

There's no personal tax to pay on dividends you receive if your total income is within the basic rate tax band (BRB). So clearly there's an advantage if you can keep your income within this limit.

But exactly how much is this? The BRB is currently £37,400. In addition there's also a tax-free "personal allowance" of £6,475. So the limit is calculated as follows:

	£
Personal allowance	6,475
Add: basic rate band	37,400
Total	43,875

If your total income, before tax, is £43,875 or below, any dividends included within it will not be liable to further tax.

Dividends are treated as paid net of 10% tax (called the "tax credit"). You must therefore add this on to the dividends you receive when working out your total income, e.g. a dividend of £900 equals gross income of £1,000. That is, £1,000 less a tax credit of 10% = £100, equates to the net dividend of £900.

If you have no other income in the tax year, so that the dividend you receive is covered by your tax-free personal allowance, you can't reclaim the tax credit on the dividend. It's better to receive a small salary or bonus to use up the personal allowance so that the tax credit attached to the dividend can then be offset against income tax.

14.3. HIGHER RATE DIVIDENDS

The amount of tax due on the dividends you receive depends on the level of your other income received in the same tax year.

14.3.1. Taxation of dividend income

TAXABLE INCOME	DIVIDEND TAX RATE
On first £37,400	10%
Between £37,400 and £150,000	32.5%
Over £150,000	42.5%

Example

In the tax year to April 5 2011 you receive dividends totalling £45,000, and no other income. The income tax due is calculated as follows:

TAXABLE INCOME	TAX DUE (£)
Dividend	45,000
Tax credit (1/9 x £40,000)	5,000
Gross dividend	50,000
Personal allowance	(6,475)
Taxable dividend	43,525
Income tax at 10% (on the first £37,400)	(3,740)
Income tax at 32.5% (on the next £6,125)	(1,991)
Offset tax credit	5,000
Tax payable	731

14.3.2. Additional income tax

£100,000 mark. From April 6 2010 your personal tax-free allowance has been subject to an income limit of £100,000. It will be reduced by £1 for every £2 of adjusted net income above the limit; with adjusted net income being broadly all income after adjustment for pension payments and charitable donations.

Example

You normally take a net dividend of £100,000 from your company and a salary equal to your personal allowance (£6,475 for both 2009/10 and 2010/11). How much more tax are you going to pay in 2010/11 compared to 2009/10? The answer is over £5,200. This is a bit of a shock as your income is nowhere near the £150,000 threshold for the new 50% tax rate.

The additional tax is due entirely to the loss of personal allowances in 2010/11, which could be preserved if you were to be able to restrict your total taxable income to below £100,000.

One solution would be to only take a net dividend of £90,000 and then top up your cash requirements with a loan from the company of up to £10,000. The tax break hinges on the hope that you can postpone paying tax on the additional £10,000 until tax rates move in a more favourable direction. However, before you take a company loan you should always talk though the tax consequences with your tax advisor.

£150,000 mark. April 6 2010 also saw the introduction of a new additional income tax rate of 50% for income above £150,000. **Note.** The dividend income is currently taxed at 10% where it falls within the basic rate band and 32.5% where liable at the higher rate of tax. A new rate of 42.5% has been introduced for dividends which fall into the income band above £150,000.

14.4. DEFERRING HIGHER RATE TAX

Tax break

As a director/shareholder you should therefore try to regulate the timing of dividends to ensure you make best use of your personal allowances, dividend lower rate bands and other reliefs. For example, it's not tax efficient to pay substantial dividends in one tax year, if you have little or no other income in an earlier and/ or later tax years. Delaying a dividend payment until after April 5 could also provide a valuable deferral of higher rate tax liability.

14.4.1. Practical points

The Taxman may challenge dividends not properly declared and paid in accordance with company law formalities. Indeed it's not possible to "backdate" a dividend - any backdated dividend (if recognised at all) will be treated as being made on the actual date of payment for tax purposes.

Company law says that once you've established the availability of distributable profits you can pay a dividend. As the owner of a company, you can decide when you take those dividends in order to minimise your tax bill. However, the Taxman may challenge the date a dividend was actually "paid" if these haven't been properly declared in accordance with company law formalities. Indeed, he can be quite picky over the actual dates of dividends, if it suits him. How can you avoid this?

There are two types of dividend, interim and final. For an interim dividend, directors have the power to pay it if it's justified by distributable profits. A final dividend must be proposed by the directors and approved by the members. The need for valid dividends is vital.

Interim dividend. Anecdotal evidence suggests that tax inspectors hold the view that an interim dividend must actually be paid to the shareholder, a credit to the loan account with the company is not sufficient. Simply holding a board meeting and preparing board minutes approving payment of an interim dividend is not enough. The Taxman specifically says: *"a board resolution recommending an interim dividend does not create an enforceable debt as it can be rescinded or varied prior to payment"*.

Why could this be a potential problem? Say your company is unable, due to cash flow constraints, to pay the interim dividend immediately in March 2011. The delay could mean the actual payment date falls into a later tax year tipping you over into higher rate tax for that year.

You can use the Taxman's own Manual against him here. This says payment is made when the money is unreservedly placed at the disposal of the shareholders as part of their current accounts with the company. So payment is made when the right to draw on the dividend exists (presumably) when the appropriate entries are made in the company's books.

TIP

Don't leave the entries in your company's books recording interim dividends until after the end of your accounting period (when the annual accounts are prepared). If you do, the due and payable date is fixed as then and not when you want it to be.

Final dividend. The due and payable date for a final dividend is the date it is approved at the general meeting (GM). It is not the date the dividend is actually paid, which can cause a problem.

Example

Say your company holds its GM on March 15 2011. At that GM the shareholders approve a final dividend up to the end of the last accounting period. However, for tax purposes you decide not to pay the dividend until April 15, i.e. you want it in the new tax year 2011/12. Unfortunately, it will be treated by the Taxman as available to you on March 15, i.e. as part of your income for the 2010/11 tax year.

TIP

At your next GM declare and approve your final dividend as usual. However, remember to specify in that approval the date when the dividend is actually going to be paid. This allows you to choose when the dividend is available to the shareholders for tax purposes.

TAX BREAK

At the end of your accounting period declare and approve a large final dividend but specify that payment is to in be equal instalments in the next accounting period. This avoids the Taxman's potential challenge of regular interim dividends.

14.5. WAIVING HIGHER RATE TAX

When a company pays a dividend, all the shareholders receive a payment in proportion to their shareholding in the company. It's a case of all or nothing. Plus, under present rules, anyone liable to the higher rate of tax suffers an additional income tax on dividends, the so-called "Schedule F upper rate". In other words, if you're already a higher rate taxpayer the problem with taking an extra dividend is that you pay tax on it, yet fellow shareholders may have no tax to pay.

TAX BREAK

Dividend waivers are often used to avoid higher rates of income tax. Broadly, a dividend waiver involves a shareholder waiving their entitlement to the dividend before the right to the dividend has accrued. A dividend waiver can therefore be used as a method of reducing the income a shareholder receives from the company.

Example

Chris and his wife Christine each own one share in Sideline Ltd (the company has only ever issued two shares). Currently, it can afford to pay a dividend of £20,000. Chris already takes a salary from another company which is sufficient to put him in higher rates of income tax and Christine is between jobs (although she does have profits from rental income of about £5,200 p.a.). Chris will pay an extra £2,500 in income tax on his share of the dividend while Christine would pay none.

If the dividend of £20,000 is voted but Chris waives his right to his share of the dividend, his £10,000 stays in the company. Christine's £10,000 still goes to her and she has no extra tax to pay on this as her total income is within the lower rate tax band of £37,400. Overall, Sideline Ltd is in the same position and the family is £2,500 better off - the tax that Chris would have paid without the waiver. The profits in the company can be taken out by Christine at a later date.

14.5.1. Practical points

1. Put the waiver in place before the right to the dividend arises or it won't work. A final dividend becomes payable once it's approved in the GM, so the deed has to be in place before then. Interim dividends must be waived before they are paid.

2. Use a formal deed to effect the waiver. It's not a complicated document. Although some people use waiver letters (formally witnessed), this is risky. Without a legal document the Taxman can still claim that the dividend is your income - so get your solicitor to check it.

3. Have genuine commercial reasons for waiving dividends. This is to avoid the Taxman treating it as some sort of bounty or gift out of income and so taxable on the shareholder waiving the dividend.

Example

Chris and Christine minuted that "a car is required in order for one shareholder/director (Christine) to obtain a new and better service for existing clients. In fact, this lack of mobility is seen as holding back the company's growth. However, following a brief discussion it was decided that this car should be bought outside the company so as to save on the employers' NI associated with a company car of the director's particular preference. At this point in the meeting (Chris) the other shareholder/ director volunteered to waive his dividend in order to allow sufficient funds to be extracted (by Christine) to purchase said vehicle privately. This was the sole condition, however, that a growth in new business could be seen to be achieved".

4. Don't waive every year as it's too obvious to the Taxman what you are doing. Use this tactic selectively. Also check that you have enough retained profits to meet the dividends in the company at the time you set up the waiver and at the time the dividends are paid - otherwise these are deemed illegal and have to be given back.

Warning. The Taxman can challenge a waiver on the basis that it constitutes a settlement for income tax purposes. This means the income would be deemed to be still yours when calculating your tax bill.

For the settlement provisions to apply an element of so-called "bounty" needs to be present. The Taxman takes the view that this is present if a dividend waiver enables one or more of the shareholders to receive a larger dividend than would have been possible if no dividend waiver had taken place. So make sure the dividend declared per share times the number of shares in issue does not exceed the amount of the company's distributable reserves.

Example

Crusty Ltd has an issued share capital of 100 ordinary shares 20% owned by Mr D and 80% by The D Children's Trust. At March 31 2010 the company has distributable profits of £100,000. If a dividend of £1,000 per share is declared and Mr D waives his entitlement before the right to the dividend accrues, there is no bounty. On the other hand, if the company declares a dividend of £1,250 per share in the knowledge that Mr D is going to waive his dividend, the Taxman will argue that bounty had occurred and under the settlement provisions Mr D would be taxed on the dividend diverted.

DIVIDEND DECLARED	£1,000 PER SHARE		£1,250 PER SHARE	
	£	£	£	£
Distributable reserves		100,000		100,000
Less dividend declared	(100,000)		(100,000)	
Add amount waived (20%)	(20,000)		(25,000)	
Dividend paid		(80,000)		(100,000)
Retained profits		20,000		-

TAX BREAK

Waiving your right to a dividend can save you higher rate tax. But the waiver must be a legal document and in place before the dividend is paid. Use this tactic sparingly to avoid unwanted attention from the Taxman. And don't pay out immediately what would have been your share of the dividend.

14.6. DIVERTING DIVIDENDS TO SAVE TAX

Most companies are formed with shares of the same class (e.g. ordinary), which means if a dividend is paid, every shareholder gets a payment, not just you. By creating different classes of share you can pay each shareholder a different dividend or nothing at all. This is what's known as a flexible dividend.

If your shares are in a class of their own (e.g. ordinary "A"), you can pay more of the company's profit to yourself rather than having to pay other shareholders or resort to paying a bonus.

When members of your family own shares in your company they can receive dividends paid in respect of those shares, as a so-called family dividend. A dividend is paid for a particular type and class of share, at the same number of pence per share to each shareholder who holds shares of that class.

Income can also be diverted from you to other members of your family by sharing the dividend. The family member may well pay less tax on the dividend than you.

14.6.1. Separate classes of share

Dividend waivers are frequently used to avoid all or part of the declared dividends going to non-passive or non-working shareholders. A more elegant solution would be to sub-divide the company's ordinary share capital into two (or more) classes of share. This would give you the flexibility to declare different dividends on each class of shares.

Some of your company's shareholders may have invested for capital growth and so do not require dividends. In practice, any conflicting requirements of shareholders over dividend policy can be satisfied by the issue of separate classes of share, with different rights as to dividends, votes and return of capital.

Example

Old School Parties Ltd has 100 ordinary shares in issue, 50 owned by Jenny, 25 by Martin and 25 by Mel. Old School Parties has enough profit to pay a dividend of £10,000 (£100 per share). As all the shares are of the same class, Jenny would receive £5,000, Martin £2,500 and Mel £2,500 (total £10,000). But the shareholders all agree that Jenny should receive more of the profits of the company because she works full-time in the business. So what Old School Parties Ltd did was to:

Step 1. *Have the shareholders hold a general meeting and agree to reclassifying the share capital so that now Jenny had 50 "A" ordinary shares, Martin 25 "B" ordinary shares and Mel 25 "C" ordinary shares.*

Step 2. *Then pay a dividend of £150 per "A" share and £50 per "B" and "C" share, so Jenny received £7,500, Martin £1,250 and Mel £1,250 (and the total dividend is still £10,000). This way Jenny received more of the profit by using a dividend.*

Reclassify the shares of your company so that each shareholder has their own class of shares. You can call them say "A" ordinary. "B" ordinary and "C" ordinary etc. until each has their own class. You can now vote a different dividend for each class of share. So if you hold the "A" shares you can take more of the profit by voting a higher dividend to the "A" shares only. You can even give a dividend to the "A" class alone.

As with most procedures involving companies, there are certain legal formalities in setting up different classes of shares. Consulting a company secretarial specialist would be wise.

Capital Gains Tax. The reorganisation of share capital is tax neutral provided each class retains the same rights. If there's a material variation in shareholders' rights, e.g. not to vote at meetings, after the reorganisation, the Taxman might levy a value-shifting charge under the Capital Gains Tax rules. In practice, provided your company is a trading company or holding company of a trading group, you should be able to make a business asset holdover election so you don't have an immediate Capital Gains Tax bill.

14.6.2. Diverting dividend income to your spouse

Some married couples and registered civil partners find that one partner pays a higher rate of tax on their income or capital gains while the other does not have enough income to even use up their personal allowance (£6,475 for 2010/11) and basic rate tax band (a further £37,400 in 2010/11). There are several ways of transferring income between partners to take advantage of these otherwise unused allowances and bands.

Your spouse can receive dividend income if they own some shares in your company. This may provide a highly tax-efficient mechanism for extracting income where the spouse has no other taxable income. It's possible to pay a dividend of up to, say, £43,875 (£37,400 + £6,475) to a non-working spouse without attracting any tax liability in the tax year ended April 5 2010.

Payment of dividends to your spouse can be achieved by: **(1)** the creation of a new class of share; or **(2)** by you transferring some of your existing shareholding to them. Depending on the facts, the Taxman may contend that such arrangements constitute a settlement. This would negate the tax advantage as the dividends would then be taxed as your income at your highest rate of tax. Similar issues may also arise with dividends paid to a civil partner on shares made available by the other partner.

14.6.3. Arctic Systems case

Tax considerations involved in securing a tax-effective dividend for your spouse have been complicated by the Taxman's publicised views and challenges in this area. Notably, the Arctic Systems case (more formally known as **Jones v Garnett**). However, this case does show that there are considerable limitations on his ability to apply the settlements legislation to shares provided to spouses of owner-managed companies.

A company was formed (Arctic Systems Ltd) which enabled Mr Jones to obtain work. Whilst his wife performed company secretarial duties for the company, she had no other involvement in the business, apart from purchasing the only other share. Over the years the company paid dividends on the shares of both Mr and Mrs Jones.

So instead of all the dividends going to Mr Jones as the sole shareholder, with him paying 40% tax on a good chunk, he was able to shift some of the dividend income to his wife by having her as the other shareholder. The tax saving comes about because (as a basic rate taxpayer) Mrs Jones didn't have any tax to pay on her share of the dividend whereas if it had gone to Mr Jones, it would have been taxed at higher rates.

If you did this in 2010/11, how much tax would it save?

Example

Tax saving on shifting income in 2010/11 is:

	TAX BILL AS BASIC RATE TAXPAYER (£)	TAX BILL AS 40% RATE TAXPAYER (£)
First 6,475 0%/40%	-	2,590
Next £37,400 at 20%/40%	7,480	14,960
Total tax	7,480	17,550

Potential tax saving of £10,070 (£17,550 - £7,480) by shifting the maximum amount of income to your spouse/partner.

By utilising another person's tax-free personal allowance for 2010/11 (£6,475) and basic rate band (up to £37,400) you could save up to £10,000 in tax.

As the situation stands at the moment, the Taxman does not have any sort of workable form of anti-income splitting legislation.

14.6.4. Providing dividend income for your children

From a legal point of view, it's possible for minor children to receive a transfer of shares in a company and be a full member and shareholder of the company (although the company has the power to refuse to register the transfer).

Children have their own personal allowances and lower/basic rate income tax bands. However, if you as their parent transfer some shares to your son or daughter, any dividend paid on these shares whilst they are an unmarried minor is taxed as if it were yours. On the other hand, it's possible for another member of the family to make a tax-effective share transfer to a minor child. The good news is that these issues don't arise where adult children hold shares.

Adult children. Once a child reaches their 18th birthday (or marries) the dividend is taxed on them (i.e. the parental settlement rule ceases to bite). A gift of shares to provide dividend income after their 18th birthday therefore offers considerable advantages. It's possible to pay a dividend of up to, say, £43,875 (£37,400 + £6,475) in 2010/11 tax-free to an individual (with no other taxable income). This is because the 10% dividend tax credit extinguishes the low tax liability on that level of income.

You may find this a less painful way of financing the increasing costs of your children's further education. The dividend income can, of course, be applied by the child for any purpose or simply saved.

TAX BREAK
_____

Any capital gain arising on the deemed market value of the gifted shares can normally to be held over or it may fall within your annual Capital Gains Tax exemption (currently £10,100).

_____

Minor children? As a general rule, shares transferred to children by other family members or friends should not be vulnerable to attack by the Taxman under the parental settlement rules, particularly if the shares have been held for a lengthy period. This will enable the dividends paid on those shares to be treated as the child's own income (invariably with no further tax liability).

TIP
_____

As a minor child can't, by law, give a valid receipt, the dividend income will be received by the parent as a bare trustee, which could be used to pay school fees.

_____

14.7. TAX RETURN ENTRIES

If you complete a tax return, the total amount of dividends you receive during a tax year should be shown under "Income from UK savings and investments". You need to collect all the vouchers for dividends paid during the tax year and add up the figures of net dividend and gross dividend and tax credit. These three totals must be included under the sub-heading "Dividends".

As a dividend is not earned income, it's ignored when calculating the maximum pension contribution that may be paid into a company pension scheme or a personal pension scheme. Although the cash received as a dividend payment may be used to pay a pension contribution, the permitted level of that contribution is calculated according to earned income such as salary and bonuses received in that tax year or in an earlier tax year (within the previous five years).

- if your total income is less than £43,875 (£6,475 + £37,400) for the tax year 2010/11, you will have no further tax to pay on dividends you receive
- however, excessive dividends can push you into higher rates of income tax and so land you with an additional income tax bill
- time the dividend payments to suit your income tax position. Obtain a longer credit period for payment of higher rate tax by paying additional dividends early in the tax year (subject to self-assessment interim payments position).

The formalities

- the amount of the dividend payment can be varied to suit the amount of profits available in the company, unlike a salary that must be paid at a similar level each month. As directors you control how much dividend is paid on a regular basis
- as a director you must always be seen to be considering the legal requirements, the company's cash flow and working capital requirements when determining the amount and timing of dividend payments
- if a dividend is paid when the company's accounts show that there was insufficient profit retained after tax to cover that dividend, the payment will be illegal under company law. An illegal dividend should be repaid. If it's not, the Taxman may argue that the payment was a loan to the shareholders.

Waiver

- a dividend can be diverted from you to other shareholders to avoid higher rates of income tax if you waive your right to receive a particular dividend payment. To do this you must submit your waiver for the dividend to the company before the shareholders approve the directors' recommendation. You cannot waive the dividend after you obtain the right to receive the dividend.

Separate classes of share

- consider sub-dividing the company's ordinary share capital into two (or more) classes of share. This would give you the flexibility to declare (different) dividends on each separate class. If your shares are in a class of their own (e.g. ordinary "A"), you can pay more of the company's profit to yourself rather than other shareholders.

Family dividends

- dividends paid to spouses who undertake significant work for the business are less susceptible to an attack from the Taxman. Particular care is required to ensure that tax-efficient dividends paid to a spouse (or civil partner) can't be challenged by the Taxman under the settlement legislation
- consider the potential advantages of paying dividends to adult children. For example, while they are away in higher education, etc. Income can be diverted from you to other members of your family by the company issuing dividends. The family member may well pay less tax on the dividend than you
- camily members can hold different classes of shares that entitle them to different rates of dividend payments. These various dividend rates can be used to reward individual family members in the most tax-efficient manner according to each person's marginal tax rate.

CHAPTER 15

Tax-efficient salaries

15.1. INTRODUCTION

Tax break

At a salary level of £110 per week (£5,720 a year) you don't pay any employees' or employers' NI, but you do get a full NI credit for the so-called Second State Pension. This pension has been designed to be generous to the lower paid so, for £5,720 per year, you get pension entitlement as if you were on £13,500. If your remuneration is below the NI threshold you don't get any entitlement to a State Pension for that year.

Why take a salary when you can draw dividends from your company? As a director/shareholder if you have no other income in the tax year you can't reclaim the tax credit on the dividend. It's better to receive a small salary or bonus to use up the personal allowance so that the tax credit attached to the dividend can then be offset against income tax.

You can also arrange for the company to pay tax-efficient salaries to other members of your family (including your spouse) in return for the work they do for it. Whether or not income tax is payable on their salary from your business depends on how much other income they receive. However, paying income tax does not detract from the benefit of the free pension credit achieved paying a salary at the level indicated above.

15.2. REVISED TAX BREAK DIVIDEND

Tax break

Dividends will be tax-free if you keep your total gross income below £43,875. Take an NI-free salary of between £4,940 and £5,720 for the tax year and top this up with dividends from company profits either from the current or previous financial years.

Having decided to take a tax efficient salary how does this affect the tax-break dividend? If you were to have no other income apart from the salary of £5,720, this would mean you could take a tax-free dividend of up to £34,339, calculated as follows:

	£
Tax-efficient income limit (£6,475 + £37,400)	43,875
Less salary	(5,720)
Allows for a gross dividend of up to	38,155
Less tax credit at 10% of gross dividend	(3,816)
Maximum tax-free dividend that can be taken	34,339

Obviously, the tax-break dividend is reduced by how much other income, e.g. from investments, rent from property etc., you have in a tax year.

Example

Kira drew a salary from her company in 2010/11 of £5,720, and received £10,000, before tax at source, bank deposit interest. Kira was able to draw a dividend of £25,339 without paying extra tax, i.e. £5,720 + £10,000 + £25,339 + 2,816 (tax credit) = £43,875. This way there is no extra tax to pay on the dividend.

15.3. NATIONAL MINIMUM WAGE ISSUE

Doesn't such a modest salary fall foul of the requirement to pay the National Minimum Wage (NMW)?

Example

£5.80 per hour for a 40-hour week for 52 weeks per year yields an annual salary of £12,064. Therefore, a salary of £5,720 (which at NMW rates is less than 19 working hours a week) may not be credible with the Taxman.

The NMW applies to all contracts of employment, even if you work for your own company. So how can you be sure you're not in breach of this legislation with possible exposure to a £5,000 fine and a criminal record? Let's look at the relationship between you (a shareholder/director) and your company in more detail.

Relationship 1. A director is an office holder. This is a statutory appointment to the board of directors for which the director may be paid for fulfilling that function. It's important to note that this does not make the director an employee of the company (even though they can do work) and therefore the NMW legislation does not apply, whatever the amount of the salary/fees.

Relationship 2. Directors of limited companies are deemed to be employees for the purpose of the NMW if they have a contract of employment. This doesn't have to be in writing but can be implied over the course of time.

15.3.1. Practical points

1. If you are one of the many paying low remuneration and high dividends, make sure the remuneration is paid to you as an "Office Holder", NOT as a worker. Have a board minute recording this. However, don't have a written contract of employment. Neither should there be any reference in any of the company's records (minutes of meetings, PAYE scheme documentation, correspondence etc.), which might enable an employer/employee relationship to be implied.

2. Don't wave a red flag! You don't need to have a letter on file stating that you do not have an employment contract. That would be unusual and might prompt further questions. Other family members who are shareholders are governed by the NMW rules if they work for the company unless they are also office holders, e.g. secretary, or even president, vice-president.

3. Record these wages and issue payslips and P60s at the end of the year - this supports what you pay. And sure enough, this is often the Taxman's next point of attack - "No payment, no deduction!" A direct debit to make sure you get paid will help here.

15.3.2. Why not take an NMW salary anyway?

Becoming a "worker" means you can get personal benefits and expenses easily classed as tax deductible in the company, under the banner of it being a legal and documented addition to your contract of employment. However, there is an, albeit small, additional tax cost of complying with the NMW at, say, a gross salary of £12,064 p.a. (£5.80 x 40 hours x 52 weeks).

15.4. FAMILY SALARIES GENERALLY

If you have control of your company, another way to extract profit from it and reduce its Corporation Tax (CT) bill at the same time is for it to pay a salary to a member of your family.

Indeed, when you start as a director with just a high salary (for pension or mortgage income purposes) and no dividend, it might be possible to reduce your own salary and pay a little bit more to the family member to reduce the total amount of income tax and NI that the family as a whole pays.

15.4.1. Why not just pay them a dividend which is NI-free?

Where shares are held by family members, the 10% tax credit on dividends can't be repaid to those who don't have sufficient other income to cover their personal allowances. If a family shareholder is in this position, your company should pay them a salary up to the level of their unused personal allowance, as well as dividends.

15.4.2. How much can your company pay?

The company must pay at least the NMW to any family member aged over 16 who works for the company. This is a minimum hourly rate that is set by law and monitored by the Taxman. The NMW rates that apply are:

Current NMW rates

AGE OF WORKER	RATE PER HOUR
16-18	£3.57
18-21	£4.83
22 and over	£5.80

In addition the company must observe the strict rules and regulations for employing children aged under 16. These rules are monitored by the Local Education Authority and limit the number of hours a child can work. Children under the age of 13 can't be employed except for light duties in very limited circumstances and it's illegal to employ a child in a factory.

15.4.3. Is the family salary tax-deductible for the company?

The Taxman will often look at the level of salary paid to family members of the company's directors. He will want to know whether the amount paid is at or above the market rate for the job. If the pay is excessive, the Taxman can argue that the reward does not reflect the work done so the payment is not wholly and exclusively made for the company's trade. In these circumstances some negotiation may be required with the Taxman to arrive at an amount that is deductible.

15.4.4. Practical points

1. The family member should be paid through the payroll just like any other employee. First, your company takes off any income tax and NI due (if any) and then pays the balance over to the family member either in the form of cash, cheque or electronic transfer to their bank account.

2. For many non-tax reasons it makes good sense to formalise a family member's employment with your company through an employment contract. For instance, if they became ill and unable to work, their contract would illustrate continuous employment and so justify a claim for Statutory Sick Pay, even if they have paid no NI contributions on their salary.

15.4.5. At what rate will they be taxed?

The rate of tax that the family member must pay on their salary from the company depends on the level of their total income for the tax year. The first £6,475 of this is tax-free. Beyond this if their income tax rate is less than yours would be, then diverting salary to them rather than you will produce income tax savings. The income tax rates on total taxable income for 2010/11 are: 20% on the first £37,400 (above £6,475) and 40% between this and £150,000 and 50% thereafter.

15.5. SPOUSE'S SALARY SPECIFICALLY

You're probably already using the tax-free personal allowance to its full advantage, e.g. as in getting the company to pay you and your spouse/partner a tax and NI-free salary of, say, £5,720, either spread over the year or a one-off bonus just before the end of the tax year.

> *Example*
>
> *Mrs X is married to a company director of a private company. In 2010/11 she works under a contract of employment for the company, for twelve hours per week at £8 per hour, and carries out a variety of functions for the company, ranging from making credit control calls (she can do this from home) to keeping personnel records up-to-date.*
>
> *Her equivalent annual salary is £5,616. This is below the NI earnings threshold and so she pays no NI and neither does the business. Also, because she has no other earnings she pays no tax.*
>
> *The business gets a full deduction for her salary against its profit, and Mrs X gets a full year's credit against her NI record that will go towards building up her right to a state pension.*

The Taxman has long been arguing that "the spouse" should only be paid a derogatory amount for any input into the business, normally this equates to the NMW. Indeed, if you employ any family members, then the rate of their remuneration will tend to come under scrutiny during the course of an enquiry into your accounts.

If you employ your spouse or partner, the traditional view is that they should be paid the same amount as you would pay a third party at arm's length; anything higher may be deemed excessive and disallowed for tax as not wholly and exclusively for the purposes of your trade.

> *Example*
>
> *The current NMW rate of £5.80 per hour, for a 35-hour week, over 52 weeks, gives a total annual salary of £10,556. However, your spouse's rate per hour might actually be higher than the NMW rate.*

For example, have a look at the rate per hour an agency would charge to provide cover (e.g. in case of illness) for your spouse's duties for the company. Even after knocking off a percentage from this for the agency's profit margin, you'll end up with a rate higher than the NMW. For example, a rate of £8 per hour would justify a £10,556 salary for only 25 hours work a week (£10,556/£8 per hour = 1,320 hours).

15.5.1. Practical points

Given the Taxman's scepticism about spouse's wages, what could your company do now? In order to head off an inspector's challenge to spouse's wages in future:

1. Even if no NI or tax has been paid, it's vital that your spouse's salary is put through the payroll system and the end-of-year certificate of pay and tax deducted (Form P14/P60) produced and submitted to the Taxman. This will ensure that your spouse's NI record is updated with a credit to go towards their pension record.

2. For many reasons it makes good sense to formalise a spouse's employment with your business through an employment contract. A job description setting out their duties wouldn't go amiss either.

3. Make separate cheque or monthly direct debit payments for the spouse's wages, which are paid into a bank account in their name (or at least into a joint account) and record this as wages in the company's cash book as if you were paying just another employee.

4. If you own two or more businesses, they may be treated as one for NI purposes by the Taxman. Thus, paying your spouse under the NI threshold at, say, £5,000 per annum from two businesses would be treated as a single salary of £10,000, which is large enough to be liable to NI.

15.5.2. Pay commission to your spouse instead

The classic method of justifying a spouse's salary is to count the hours worked and multiply them by the NMW. However, there are alternative approaches that might suit your business better.

Let's say your spouse advertises the business by word of mouth. Is the spouse then not entitled to a commission on every client they introduce to the company? And in turn can that commission not be a percentage of the work done? The answer is "Yes" and "Yes" as long as the transaction is recorded properly, it's difficult for the Taxman to challenge the validity of such a payment.

The important point is that whatever you do, document and log everything. For example, you could keep a spreadsheet of how the final commission figure was calculated. The Taxman then has to look at your business on the facts unique to it. He can't then rely on his long list of case law to please himself and declare what has been paid to your spouse as being excessive and not related to the trade.

You can even have different commission rates for different products or services. For example, the referral scheme commission payments offered by one small IT company were 50% of website hosting costs; 15% of Internet marketing services; and 10% of web design and development costs. And no matter how small the project, they'd still make a minimum commission payment of £50.

TAX BREAK

If "hours x NMW rate" can't justify your spouse's salary, then try calculating commission due to them regarding work/clients introduced by them to your company. This will help to justify the level of any regular payment they receive from the company should it be challenged by the Taxman.

15.6. PENSION CONTRIBUTION ON A LOW SALARY

Does a tax break exist where directors and/or their spouses can be paid a basic "personal allowance" salary and then have massive pension contributions paid by their company to their pension scheme? Provided their overall package is at a market rate, an employee/director can legitimately have both a salary and a pension contribution paid by their company. As part of the cost of employing staff, pension contributions will, at first look, be tax deductible for the company.

However, it's worth noting the Taxman's view, which is that the pension contribution is deductible *"in respect of... an employee who is a close relative... of the director or if it is comparable with that paid to unconnected employees performing duties of similar value."* So how much pension can your company pay to extract profits through this route?

Example

Mr J is a director of a small company, and employs his spouse for general administration work. A modest salary of £1,200 a year is paid, which is easily commensurate with the duties she carries out. The company also pays an employer contribution into a personal pension scheme for her of £100 per month.

Mr J's pension's advisor is insisting that the company is perfectly entitled to full tax relief on all of the £1,200 annual contributions actually paid, irrespective of the salary earned, and is seeking to persuade Mr J's company to increase the pension contributions to the maximum £300 per month (£3,600/12) and obtain maximum Corporation Tax relief.

One trick to justifying a one-off higher contribution is to focus on the number of years that the spouse has worked for the company without a pension scheme. If the annual premium going down this route is not significant, it might be because there haven't been many years of service pre-pension. However, you could link a "one-off" pension contribution for the spouse (in our example £3,600 - £1,200 = £2,400) by the company to a year of higher profits and record them as a reward for helping to earn those profits. This should pass the Taxman's "wholly and exclusively" test for tax deductibility. However, don't do this every year.

TAX BREAK

Any amount up to £3,600 per year may be paid as personal pension contributions, but that doesn't mean that the premiums are necessarily tax deductible for the company. Get your advisor to come up with a figure to justify the current pension contribution by taking into account the number of years of service (and salary paid in those years) before this pension arrangement was thought up.

TAX BREAK

Your company can make regular contributions as long as it's what other employees might receive and it relates to making up for past years' service. As a one-off you could pay a performance-related contribution for a spouse on a low salary.

15.7. TEEN WAGES

Have you ever stopped to think how much your teenager's pocket money costs you? With two offspring aged, say, 13 and 15, funding their teenage spending habits could be burning through nearly £2,000 per year of your gross income, and that's before you take into account the cost of their mobile phone bills and providing a "free" taxi service for them!

For example:

		£
15-year-old:	£12.50 x 52 weeks	£650
13-year-old:	£10 x 52 weeks	£520
Total cash per year		£1,170
Tax and NI at your 41% marginal rate (including NI at 1%)		£813
Your gross salary required		£1,983

They will have to work for their money of course, but every Saturday morning spent in profitable employment at your company may teach them something about the family business as well as clear those little jobs that are always left undone. For example: filing, data-entry, cleaning the company vans/cars, sweeping-up, shelf-stacking or counting stock. A 14-year-old can achieve quite a lot with the minimum of training. As long as the task is safe and doesn't require heavy lifting it's perfectly legal to employ children aged over twelve. Instead of paying the weekly £10 out of your own pocket, get your company to pay them a wage.

The company will get tax relief for the full amount of their wages, and you get to keep more of your own after-tax personal income.

They have their own tax-free personal allowance of £6,475 (for 2010/11) to use, which should cover all their Saturday morning earnings leaving nothing to tax under PAYE. There will be no NI to pay either as children aged under 16 do not have to pay NI and employers don't have to pay NI for them either.

15.7.1. Practical points

1. Put the teenagers on the company payroll as regular employees. To do this properly you should help them complete the Form P46, as they will be employed for more than one week (hopefully!).

2. Although they are too young to pay NI, you should ask the Taxman to issue an NI number for them so that your company can complete the end-of-year PAYE forms correctly. Until this permanent NI number is issued, you can use a temporary number but that needs to be replaced before the tax year-end.

3. As your offspring are now regular employees of the company, it can provide them with benefits-in-kind such as mobile phones. Remember, the company must own the phone and sign the contract with the provider to make the phone tax-free.

4. There is a legal minimum wage set for those aged 16 to 18 of £3.57 per hour. You don't have to pay as much as that to someone younger than 16, but it's a good guide.

5. The hours worked mustn't take up school time, and can't be before 7am or after 7pm. As a prospective employer of children, you may also need to ask your local authority about permits, even to employ your own child.

TAX BREAK

For their "Saturday job" put the teenager on your company payroll as a regular employee. This is more tax efficient than paying them out of your already taxed income. They will, of course, have to work for their money.

- even if you are using dividends to extract most of the profit from your company, take a salary of either £5,720 or one meeting the NMW requirement (for example £12,064) in the tax year 2010/11
- drawing a salary of between £95 and £110 per week, which is a maximum of £5,720 for 2010/11 means that neither you nor your company will be due to pay any NI. But your earnings will count towards your state pension as if NI had been paid.

National Minimum Wage (NMW) issue

- a director who is only an office holder under the Companies Act, is not a worker under the NMW. However, a director who is a worker must be paid at least the NMW rates. The adult rate is currently £5.80 per hour
- make sure there's no evidence, e.g. an employment contract, to suggest that an employer/employee relationship exists. You are then being paid a salary as an office holder (e.g. a director) and so the NMW does not apply.

Family salary

- a salary paid to a family member may be taxed at a lower rate than it would be if it were paid as part of your salary
- a salary of £110 per week or less paid to a family member is free of NI
- reasonable salaries paid to family members are tax-deductible for the company, and can reduce the level of Corporation Tax paid by it
- the family member must perform some real work for the company to justify the reward of a salary, and the company must pay an adult family member an amount that is at least equal to the NMW for the hours worked
- the NMW set for those aged 16 to 18 of £3.57 per hour. You don't have to pay as much as that to someone younger than 16, but it's a good guide. The hours worked mustn't take up school time, or be before 7am or after 7pm.

Pension contributions

- as well as salary, a payment could be made as an employer's contribution to a partner's personal pension plan. The partner will not be taxed on this benefit nor will NI be payable on it
- like salary, the pension payments will be deductible from business profits provided the salary and the pension payment combined do not exceed a reasonable rate of remuneration for the work carried out. Excessive pension contributions for a partner or relative may not be deductible on the grounds that they are not wholly and exclusively for the purpose of the trade.

CHAPTER 16

Director's loan account

16.1.　INTRODUCTION

You can use a bit of imagination here and get your personal expenditure into the company as business expenses by utilising your director's loan account (DLA).

A DLA typically arises when a company is set up and the shareholders/directors put their own funds into the company as start-up capital. The company now owes this money to the directors and the funds are available to be withdrawn as and when required, subject to the cash being available.

Example

Calum started as a self-employed designer in April 2006. By 2010 he was employing several other designers. His accountant advised him to incorporate the business. Its reputation (goodwill) was valued at £100,000 and so the new company credited Calum's DLA with that sum. The company can claim Corporation Tax relief on the £100,000, even though it hasn't actually paid over any cash.

At other times, if your company can't afford to pay all of your salary or dividends at once, you can leave them in your DLA and draw down on the tax-free funds whenever you want to.

16.2.　CHARGING EXPENSES

The DLA can be used as a mechanism for the introduction of expenses into the company:

Example

Simon, who is a director of his company, spent £700 of his own money entertaining business customers and fills in an expenses claim. But because all of the company's spare cash is tied up in working capital, Simon decides not to draw the £700 from the company just yet. However, because he's spent money on company business he knows he can credit the sum to his DLA and charge the corresponding expense to entertaining in the accounts. The £700 is now owed to Simon and he can claim it at a later date.

TAX BREAK

By crediting an amount to your DLA you can simply withdraw the cash tax-free at a later date.

If you are a little short on the required sum in your private bank account and the company is in funds, then it's perfectly legal for the company to pay for a director's or employee's holiday, for example, as long as you transfer the costs to reduce your DLA and not try to pass them off as a business expense. But remember, this is only a temporary solution as the loan will have to be repaid in due course.

16.2.1. Practical points

As with everything, you must have adequate records to support your claim. So, for example, if it's a credit for an entertaining expense you are seeking, this means keeping receipts, bar bills, credit card vouchers etc. This may seem like a chore but the more documentation you can gather, the stronger your case.

However, there are no special rules to worry about here. The documentation kept in support of your claim forms part of the company's books in the same way any other expenses invoices do. Unlike putting an entry on your tax return or on a P11D, these claims are not separately identifiable from the rest of the company's day-to-day expenses which will eventually appear in the annual accounts.

This doesn't mean they won't ever be queried by the Taxman. They could be picked up or challenged through an enquiry into the company's tax return or on a compliance visit.

Advantages of charging expenses to your DLA include:

- it's simple and straightforward with no P11Ds or entries on your tax return to worry about
- you don't need to have prior approval from the Taxman to get the expense reimbursed
- there's no "necessarily" test to comply with to claim a tax deduction
- you always get a full tax-free reimbursement and it can be drawn as and when required
- the company gets a full deduction as appropriate.

16.2.2. What type of expenses can you credit to your DLA?

The simple answer is: anything and everything, so long as it has been "wholly and exclusively" incurred for the purposes of your company's trade. (The "necessarily" part doesn't apply here because it's an ordinary business expense not an employee expense.) So it's not just entertaining you can claim for. It could be a "use of home" claim for doing the books on the kitchen table, calculated as a percentage of your household bills or perhaps a mileage expense using the appropriate tax-free rates.

16.3. CHARGING INTEREST

When the company borrows from a bank it must pay interest on the money advanced. If you have a DLA with the company that's in credit, i.e. the company is holding money that is due to you, you are also effectively lending money to it. You can ask the company to pay you interest on the credit balance of your DLA, and on any other funds you have lent to it.

The extraction of funds is often influenced by a company's cash flow position; indeed, shareholders often loan funds back to the company to restore liquidity and provide working capital. This creates a loan to the company or a credit balance on a DLA, on which there is nothing to stop directors charging interest.

Example

Mr F is a 75% shareholder of Full Security Service Ltd. Over the years he has ploughed back part of his dividend income to provide working capital for his company. During the company's year ended December 31 2010 the balance outstanding on his loan account with the company was £100,000 on which he charged interest at the rate of 6% per annum. Interest due to him from the company is therefore £6,000. His company pays Corporation Tax (CT) at the rate of 21%. So being able to include this interest in its year-end accounts would reduce its CT bill payable in October 2011. The tax position for the company and Mr F is as follows:

COMPANY	£
Taxable profits before interest	150,000
Less interest charge	(6,000)
Taxable profit after interest charge	144,000
Corporation Tax (CT) at 21%	(30,240)
Profit after tax	113,760
Company tax saving on interest £6,000 x 21%	1,260
MR F	£
Interest received net of tax deducted by the company	
£6,000 less £1,200 (£6,000 x 20%)	4,800
Less income tax payable	
£6,000 at 40% = £2,400 less £1,200 (tax deducted at source by the company)	(1,200)
Net amount received	3,600

A company normally obtains relief for interest charged in its accounts on an accruals basis, i.e. the amount charged against its profits. So it can claim a tax deduction for interest accrued for the shareholder but not yet paid. However, any loan in a close company (the controlling parties must number no more than five) from a shareholder, or an associate of a shareholder, is subject to the "late interest rule". This means that the CT deduction for any interest that remains unpaid more than twelve months after the accounting period end is deferred until interest is actually paid.

So the company will get relief for the interest on a loan from a shareholder on an accruals basis if it is paid within twelve months after the end of the relevant accounting period.

Example

The company will obtain tax relief for the year ended December 31 2010 provided the interest is paid to Mr F by December 31 2011. However, CT relief will not be given if the interest is simply "rolled up" as a credit to his loan account and remains outstanding at December 31 2012.

The recipient shareholder/director is taxed on the gross interest received, with credit being given for any tax deducted at source by the company.

TAX BREAK

There's no employees' NI due on interest paid to you by the company, as it doesn't constitute earnings, as long as the rate used is not in excess of a commercial one.

16.3.1. Paying the interest

1. The interest can be paid by cheque or by electronic transfer to your personal bank account or credited to your director's loan account (thereby increasing the balance owed by the company to you).

2. The payment can be made on a regular basis, either monthly or quarterly, or annually if you wish. However, as the company has to tell the Taxman how much interest it has paid to you each quarter, it may be convenient for it to pay the interest due to you on the same basis.

3. In order to help you with your tax affairs the company should issue you with an annual certificate of interest for the relevant tax year.

TAX BREAK

The commercial rate could be several points above bank base rate. This would recognise that it may become a risk if the company gets into financial difficulty.

4. The company should pay a commercial rate of interest on the money it has borrowed from you. This may be 5% or 6% over the bank base rate. However, if the company pays more than a commercial rate, the Taxman may view the excess as a payment of salary and require the company to deduct income tax and NI from it.

16.3.2. Tax return entries

The interest you receive from the company must be shown on your tax return, under "Income from UK savings and investments". You should copy the amount of net interest paid from the certificate provided by the company, to your tax return. You are also required to enter the amount of tax deducted and the gross amount of interest paid before tax.

16.3.3. Can you deduct any expenses from this interest?

If you have borrowed from a bank to lend money to the company, the interest you're charged by the lender can be deducted as an expense on your tax return, but only if the following conditions apply:

1. The company must be a close company which means it is controlled by its directors or there are five or fewer shareholders.

2. The company must either be trading or control a company that is trading, or it must hold land that is let to someone connected with the company.

3. You must own at least 5% of the company's shares or be able to control at least 5% of the shares through your relatives or associates at the time the interest is paid.

16.3.4. At what rate will your interest be taxed?

The tax you pay on interest received from the company will depend on the level of your other income in the same tax year. The interest is taxed after taking account of salary/bonuses but before adding dividends to your total income. If the company has already deducted income tax at 20%, you don't have to pay any further tax as a basic rate (20%) taxpayer. If you pay tax at a higher rate, e.g. 40%, you will have to pay further income tax at the rate of 20% on the interest received.

16.4. OVERDRAWN LOAN ACCOUNTS

Let's say you take a modest monthly salary from your company and receive an annual dividend once the profit for the year is finalised. But when large bills crop up, such as car repairs or a holiday deposit, the company picks up the tab and charges the cost to your DLA, which causes your loan account to slide into the red for a few months.

When your loan account goes overdrawn by more than £5,000, the Taxman says that you are getting the benefit of an interest-free loan. You need to either pay interest on that loan at the official rate (4.75%), or pay tax on the estimated interest. If your account is overdrawn by, say, £10,000 for six months, the interest due is £237.50 (£10,000 x 4.75% x 6/12). The tax payable at 40% amounts to £95 (£237.5 x 40%) - not much to worry about. The company is also stung with Class 1A NI at 12.8% on the estimated interest, which totals £30 (£237.5 x 12.8%), but again that won't break the bank.

Your accountant probably sorts this out for you at the year-end, by either getting the company to vote you a bonus or allocating some of the annual dividend to your DLA. Either way, the account is written back to zero, and everyone's happy - except the Taxman.

16.4.1. Advance payments of salary

The Taxman has been known to say that any personal expenses charged to your loan account are advance payments of salary, so you and the company have to pay Class 1 NI at the time these amounts are credited to your loan account.

Example

The company paid your car repair bill of £3,500 on May 1 2010 and your holiday deposit of £2,000 on June 1 2010. The NI due is:

BILL PAID	NI DUE	
	Employers' NI	*Employees' NI*
£3,500 on 1/5/10	£448 (£3,500 x 12.8%)	£385 (£3,500 x 11%)
£2,000 on 1/6/10	£256 (£2,000 x 12.8%)	£220 (£2,000 x 11%)
Total	£704	£605

If you don't pay the NI until the Taxman audits the company in August 2011, interest will be due on the late payment of the total NI. He will also try to charge a penalty for your error.

Intention is the key here. If your intention was always to clear the account with a dividend or personal funds, the expenses making up the overdrawn balance can't be earnings and are not subject to Class 1 NI.

16.4.2. Practical points

1. Get the company to minute its policy regarding overdrawn DLAs; that those accounts must be cleared by a dividend or personal funds introduced by the director, and are not intended to be advances on directors' salary due.

2. If the Taxman refuses to agree with you, refer him to his own leaflet, "NI for Company Directors". This says: *"No liability for NI on the overdrawn amount, or the increase in the overdrawn amount, if the withdrawal is made in anticipation of an introduction of funds which are not earnings, for example, dividends, matured insurance policies or other personal income."*

16.4.3. Clearing an overdrawn DLA

If the DLA is not returned to credit within nine months of your company's year-end, s.419 of the **Taxes Act 1988** imposes an additional Corporation Tax (CT) charge of 25% on the amount which remains overdrawn. The tax is not refunded until the due date for the payment of CT, in respect of the period in which the loan is cleared. This amounts to a significant period of time to be deprived of funds. The tax charge and the loss of funds continue all the while the matter is not addressed. So the price of inaction can become relatively expensive.

Clearly, the loan will need to be repaid or the tax consequences suffered, and when it comes to using the profits in the company, there are two main options:

Option 1. Additional salary. To work out how much gross salary you would need to pay yourself to clear the DLA, work out (amount of cheque/59) x 100 (if you are a 40% taxpayer). For a 20% taxpayer it's (amount of cheque/69) x 100. Don't forget the company pays employers' NI on the additional salary at 12.8%.

Option 2. Additional dividend. Taking a dividend and using this to clear the DLA would, of course, save on NI (both employees' and employers') compared to salary.

> *Example*
>
> *When checking your March 31 2010 company's draft accounts in order to prepare your 2009/10 income tax return, your advisor finds that your director's account was overdrawn by just under £1,000. Although you're not talking about a large amount of money, what is the most tax efficient way of dealing with this situation?*
>
> *At present, the overdrawn loan account is only £1,000 and so there is no benefit-in-kind to consider as it's less than £5,000. Consequently, you are only comparing the tax impact of a dividend or paying tax under s.419. If the shareholder (you) is a higher rate taxpayer, the effective rate of tax is 25%. A dividend of £1,000 is grossed up at 90% to £1,111. Taxed at 32.5% this is £361. After the tax credit of £111, the additional tax payable under self-assessment is £250 (subject to rounding for pence), i.e. 25% of £1,000. Tax under s.419 is 25% of the loan, i.e. £250.*

Therefore, if you are comparing tax on a dividend with tax on a loan, there's no difference apart from timing. The loan will need to be repaid at some point and so, in normal circumstances, the question is whether to pay a dividend to be taxed through self-assessment, payable on January 31 after the year-end, or s.419 tax on January 1 after the year-end (for a March 31 year-end). The s.419 tax will be refunded after the loan account has been repaid but even then only when the company's next accounting period has been agreed.

If you can then draw an extra dividend and use this to clear your loan account. If your loan account is not returned to credit within nine months of your company's year-end, the Taxman imposes a 25% tax charge. In terms of cash flow, payment of personal tax on an additional dividend is better than repaying 100% of the loan account from private funds; profits permitting of course.

16.4.4. Practical points

1. Once the company has paid you, pay it back. This is less open to attack from a picky inspector rather than just having a bookkeeping entry cancelling out the DLA and arguing when that entry was made.

2. When clearing a loan account always add that extra £1 and put it back into credit, don't just clear it down to zero. This way you prove beyond doubt to the Taxman that you cleared the loan account on a particular date.

3. Even if your company is a secondary source of income for you and, in the past, you have left earnings in the company taking no salary or dividends, be aware of the overdrawn loan account trap.

16.4.5. Writing off the loan balance

TAX BREAK

You don't have to pay a dividend to clear a loan account. Reorganise the accounts amongst the directors and then write the loans off. If the Taxman challenges this tactic, politely point to his own manual that allows it!

The classic solution on an overdrawn DLA is to pay the money back to the company, or as is more usual, taking extra remuneration from the company in the form of dividends or bonuses to cover the overdraft. Most people take a dividend to save on NI, however, there can be a problem with this.

Example

Mr and Mrs S hold shares in their company, 75:25 in favour of Mr S. His income is just below the threshold for paying 40% income tax. Mrs S's income, on the other hand, is well within the basic rate tax band of 20%. The couple decide to borrow £15,000 from their company.

Why £15,000? Because Mrs S only owns 25% of the shares, the total company dividend has to be £30,000 for her to receive £7,500 (£30,000 x 25%). However, this means that Mr S would be faced with a tax bill of £5,625 on his share of the extra dividend.

Tax law says that if a loan of this type is discharged or written off by the company, then it is treated in the same way as if it were a dividend paid to that individual. The proportion of shareholdings are irrelevant; what matters is the amount written off.

> *Example*
>
> *Mrs S's extra dividend income from the write-off would be £15,000 x 100/90 = £16,667. The extra £1,667 is classed as a tax credit, and gets deducted from the final tax bill. If the director/shareholder is a basic rate taxpayer, then just like with dividends, there's no further tax to pay.*

16.4.6. Practical points

1. Plan ahead, making sure you take advantage of any lower rate band available by splitting the loan between different shareholders.

2. Formalise the loan in advance by getting a company minute drawn up. This helps if there are any queries raised by the Taxman in the future.

3. Include the grossed-up amount written off in your personal tax return. The Tax Return Guide on the Taxman's website includes step-by-step instructions.

Note. Higher rate taxpayers would have to pay extra tax at the year-end on a dividend arising from a loan write-off. The advantage over a dividend is that you don't have to find the money to physically clear the loans.

16.4.7. Get your dates right

You can choose when to take dividends in order to clear your DLA. However, the Taxman may challenge the date a dividend was actually "paid" if it hasn't been properly declared in accordance with company law formalities. Indeed, he can be quite picky over the dates of dividends, if it suits him. How can you avoid hassle over dividend dates?

Anecdotal evidence suggests that many tax inspectors still hold the misguided belief that an interim dividend must actually be paid to the shareholder; a credit to the loan account with the company is not sufficient. Simply holding a board meeting and preparing board minutes approving payment of an interim dividend is also not enough. The Taxman says: *"A board resolution recommending an interim dividend does not create an enforceable debt as it can be rescinded or varied prior to payment."*

Why could this be a potential problem? Say your company is unable, due to cash flow constraints, to pay the interim dividend immediately in March 2011. The delay could mean the actual payment date falls into a later tax year which may be undesirable if this pushes you into higher rate tax for that year.

You can use the Taxman's own Manual against him here. This says payment is made when the money is unreservedly placed at the disposal of the directors/ shareholders as part of their current accounts with the company. So payment is made when the right to draw on the dividend exists (presumably) when the appropriate entries are made in the company's books.

TIP

Don't leave any entries in your company's books recording interim dividends until after the end of your accounting period (until, say, the annual accounts are being prepared). If you do, the due and payable date is fixed as then and not when you want it to be.

16.4.8. DLAs and the new tax penalty regime

As your DLA record-keeping and accounting procedures could impact on what you report on your next tax return, they could be subject to the Taxman's new penalty regime. The penalty for a deliberate inaccuracy can range from between 20% and 100%. The highest penalties being reserved for those cases involving concealment of information or evidence. By contrast, if you can prove that you have taken proper and reasonable care in preparing your tax return, then the Taxman will consider any error an innocent one and charge no penalty at all. The importance of good record-keeping is therefore vital.

The Taxman has published guidance on the new penalty rules in his Compliance Handbook, including examples of what he considers to be deliberate errors. Some of these examples are worryingly easy to envisage occurring in owner-managed businesses because the distinction between where the owner's personal finances end and the business' begin are blurred.

One example given by the Taxman of deliberate but not concealed inaccuracies is withdrawing money for personal use from a limited company and not making an attempt to ensure it's treated correctly for tax purposes.

If, as is common, you draw money from the company via your DLA that is later repaid by a bonus or dividend, this could lead to a penalty because the loan potentially creates a taxable benefit-in-kind. This is despite the usual practice to ignore the loan if it's repaid within the tax year. The Taxman has indicated that he would consider this a deliberate error. The penalty could be as much as 70% of the tax involved.

The Taxman also gives examples of concealed inaccuracies, such as describing expenditure in the business records in such a way as to make it appear to be business-related when it is in fact private. If you buy a personal item using the company bank account and your bookkeeper incorrectly records it as a business expense because it's something that the business might usually purchase, this may be construed as concealment by the Taxman. This could lead to a penalty of 70% or more of the tax involved.

16

> **TIP**
>
> If the money you withdraw from your company will ultimately become salary/bonus or dividends, then record it as such straightaway.

> **TIP**
>
> Have a system for identifying personal expenses so that your bookkeeper doesn't enter them as business costs.

16.5.   KEEPING YOUR OWN RECORDS

It's quite common for an inspector to ask to be provided with an analysis of the DLAs. The Taxman will then look in detail at whether or not what purports to be a credit for a dividend or a debit for an expense was actually made on the date it said it was.

Where, as is usual, the company's advisor writes up the books, the date of entries on a loan account will be the one on which the books are written up and the relevant entries posted to the loan account. If the purpose of declaring a dividend was to clear an overdrawn loan account, then that loan account could remain overdrawn for longer, if you just rely on a once-a-year balance, with all the consequences that follow.

> **TIP**
>
> If your books are written up infrequently, keep a director's loan account worksheet to record all of your transactions with the company. Record date, description and amount in (+) or out (-) when it occurs.

> **TIP**
>
> Strike a balance (add up the +s and -s) on the paper each month to avoid the consequences of an overdrawn loan account.

Charging expenses
- the DLA can be used as a mechanism for the introduction of expenses into the company. By crediting an amount to your DLA you can simply withdraw the cash tax-free at a later date
- Anything and everything can be charged, so long as it has been "wholly and exclusively" incurred for the purposes of your company's trade.

Charging interest
- there's no NI due on the interest paid to you by the company
- you can charge the company a commercial interest rate on the funds it holds on your behalf, or the money you lend to it. That interest rate will be higher than the rate you would receive from a bank or building society if you deposited the same funds with those institutions
- if the interest is paid at a rate in excess of a reasonable commercial one, the Taxman will demand that income tax and NI be deducted by the company from the excess
- the company can deduct the interest it pays you from its profits before Corporation Tax is payable
- you can withdraw the capital from the company on which the interest is paid at any time, with no tax consequences.

Overdrawn DLAs
- the classic solution on an overdrawn DLA is to pay the money back to the company, or as is more usual, taking extra remuneration from the company in the form of dividends or bonuses to cover the overdraft
- get the company to minute its policy regarding overdrawn DLAs; that those accounts must be cleared by a dividend or personal funds introduced by the director, and are not intended to be advances on directors' salary due
- you don't have to pay a dividend to clear a loan account. Reorganise the accounts amongst the directors and then write the loans off.

Keeping records
- in company tax enquiry cases it's quite common for the inspector to ask to be provided with an analysis of the DLAs
- if your books are written up infrequently, keep a director's loan account worksheet to record all of your transactions with the company. Record date, description and amount in (+) or out (-) of a transaction when it occurs. Strike a balance (add up the +s and -s) each month to avoid the consequences of an overdrawn loan account.

CHAPTER 17

As your company's landlord

17.1. INTRODUCTION

A number of director/shareholders leave their personally owned property outside the company to mitigate the effect of a potential double tax charge: firstly, when the company eventually sells the property and secondly when they try to extract the proceeds from that sale. Holding property outside the company (hopefully) creates wealth, free from claims of creditors, etc.

In such cases the director can extract funds from the company by charging it a market rent for the use of the property. The rent is normally paid under a formal lease agreement between the two parties. If the property is jointly owned, for example by the director and their spouse, then the rent would be paid to both in the appropriate ownership shares.

The rent paid by the company is tax deductible against its profits (provided that it represents a market rent) and the rent received is taxable in the director's hands as property income. However, no NI liability arises. The director can deduct, as a property business expense, the normal expenses of running a let property.

Where the director/shareholder has borrowed money to purchase the property, they would normally charge rent to secure immediate tax relief for that interest.

Clearly, if only part of the building is let, then only the corresponding part of the costs can be deducted as a property business expense.

Other allowable expenses include capital allowances on plant attached to the building.

> **TAX BREAK**
>
> The tax effect of extracting profits via a rent is similar to the payment of remuneration, except that no PAYE or NI is payable.

17.2. CHARGING RENT

Rent is a sum you receive from the company in return for allowing it to use property you own. The property may be a commercial or a domestic building, land, or even part of a building. On a smaller scale, even if your company uses the garage attached to your home, e.g. to store stock, you can let it out and receive rent in return.

The rent should normally be paid under a formal lease agreement between you and the company. This agreement will stipulate how often the rent should be paid, either monthly, quarterly or annually.

The company should pay the rent by giving you a cheque for the amount due or by making an electronic transfer to your private bank account.

If, as a private individual, you enter into such a contract with your company, you should tell all the other directors at a board meeting. The minutes of the meeting should record when the lease agreement is due to start and how much will be paid under it.

If the property is jointly owned, say, by you and your spouse, the rent should be paid to you both. Alternatively, you can receive all the rent on behalf of the other owner or owners and pay out the proportion which is due to them.

You can leave the rent due to you in your director's loan account. This can help the company with its cash flow, and the delayed withdrawal has no tax consequences for you or your company.

You can charge the company as little rent as you wish for using your property. However, if the rent is not enough to cover the expenses connected with the property, such as repairs and insurance, you will lose money. Any loss you make from letting property can only be set against profits from letting in the future; it can't be used to reduce tax due on your other income in the same or earlier years.

If the lease is for a significant sum compared to the other expenses of the company, the amount paid will have to be shown in the notes to your company's annual accounts.

Rent-a-room relief. Letting a room in your own home is normally tax-free if the total rent received in a tax year is less than £4,250. Unfortunately, this tax relief does not apply if the room is used by a business for an office or for storage. However, if the room is used by the company to provide accommodation to an employee, the rent-a-room relief does apply.

Jointly owned. If the property is owned with another person, you should only report the portion of the rent and expenses on your tax return that relates to your share. However, if you own the property jointly with your spouse you normally have to share the income equally, whatever your actual share in the property. If you declare your actual ownership in the property, you can divide the rent and expenses along those lines.

Example

You contributed £10,000 to buy a property whilst your spouse paid £40,000. The property is let to your company for £5,000 per year and there are £1,000 worth of expenses relating to the letting. You and your spouse should each show rents received of £2,500 on your respective tax returns and expenses of £500, even if all the rent is paid to you and you meet all the costs.

If you both sign an election telling the Taxman the actual percentage of the property you each own, you can split the rent with £1,000 shown on your tax return and £4,000 on your spouse's. The expenses should be divided in the same way.

17.3. ENTRIES ON YOUR TAX RETURN

The rent you receive from the company is income from land or property. If the property is in the UK, you should include the rent on "Land and Property" supplementary pages with your tax return. If the property is abroad, e.g. a villa in Spain, you should fill in details of the rents received and expenses set against that rent on the "Foreign Income" supplementary pages.

If you have not received a tax return, or a notice reminding you to complete it electronically, you must ask the Taxman to set a record up for you on his self-assessment system. If you receive rent for the first time and do not normally complete a tax return, you must tell him by October 5 after the end of the tax year when you started to receive the rent.

17.4. EXPENSES YOU CAN DEDUCT FROM THE RENT

You can deduct any expenses from the rent which are wholly and exclusively connected with the land or building that is being let. These expenses may include:

- interest paid on a loan used to buy or improve the property

- repairs to the building (but not the cost of improvements)

- cost of services such as water rates (if the tenant doesn't pay them directly)

- legal costs of drawing up a short-term lease

- buildings insurance

- capital allowances on any plant or equipment fixed to the building

- security guards to protect the property (if you pay for these yourself)

- accountancy fees for working out your profit after deductions.

If you let part of a building to the company, but pay all the main services, you should set a proportion of those costs against the rent received.

Example

You occupy the upper two floors of a three-storey property, while your company trades from the ground floor. The total cost of the mortgage interest, buildings insurance, heating and lighting should be apportioned so that one-third is deducted as an expense from the rent the company pays to you.

You may feel that the company is responsible for more than one third of the total electricity bill, because it uses powerful lighting or industrial air heaters in the retail space on the ground floor. If this is the case you should split the costs on a reasonable basis and make a note of how you reached that apportionment in case the Taxman ever asks you to justify your calculations.

17.4.1. At what rate will the rent finally be taxed?

The rate of income tax that applies to the rent less expenses depends on your total income during the tax year.

17.5. RENTING EXAMPLE

Example

Mr L owns the entire share capital of Ilamps Ltd. The factory it uses, however, was originally purchased by Mr and Mrs L in equal shares. For the year ended March 31 2011 the company is charged a rent of £30,000. Mr and Mrs L's claim for capital allowances for the year was £3,000 each and their other allowable property expenses were £2,000 each.

The company's taxable profits for the year ended March 31 2011 were £260,000 before charging the rent.

	COMPANY	MR L	MRS L
	£	£	£
Taxable profits before rent	260,000		
Less rent charged	(30,000)	15,000	15,000
Taxable profit after rent charge	230,000		
Less Corporation Tax at 21%	(48,300)		
Post-tax profit	181,700		
Less capital allowances		(3,000)	(3,000)
Allowable expenses		(2,000)	(2,000)
Taxable rent		10,000	10,000
Corporation Tax saving on rent			
£30,000 x 21%	6,300		
Income tax payable			
At marginal tax rate of 40%		4,000	
At marginal tax rate of 20%			2,000

17.6. RECOVERING VAT

You don't automatically charge VAT on top of the rent you charge the company. However, you might end up with some irrecoverable input VAT suffered on the cost of acquiring the building originally and/or refurbishing it, if you don't. The rule is no VAT charge, no VAT recovery!

TAX BREAK

Providing the building is used for commercial purposes (not a residential property), you can register for VAT and opt to tax it, which means charging VAT on the rent. However, you are now able to recover all the VAT on your costs. Of course, this means completing a VAT return on a regular basis and paying any VAT you owe.

Once registered for VAT and having opted to tax the building, you will have to charge VAT on any service charges you bill the company for.

Provided your company does not make exempt supplies, it can recover the VAT on the rent if you charge it.

17.6.1. What's the best thing to do?

Scenario 1. If you've been charged substantial VAT on acquiring the building or incur significant input VAT on expenditure to the building, e.g. during a refurbishment, then register for VAT and opt to tax and recover the VAT now. If the company is able to recover the VAT that you charge it, then there's no loss to anybody, the VAT just moves around in a circle but you have also recovered the VAT that you incurred.

Scenario 2. The same situation as above but the company can't recover some or all of the VAT that it's charged. Over time you will hand back the VAT you have recovered as output tax on the rents, but this can take a long time. Meanwhile, a significant cash flow advantage is achieved.

Scenario 3. If your VAT costs are small, don't bother to opt to tax. There is no cash flow advantage in this situation.

17.7. INTEREST ONLY

Instead of charging a rent, the director could arrange for the company to pay the interest on their personal borrowings that have been taken out to purchase or improve the property. Such "interest" is deductible in computing the company's trading profits as it represents compensation for occupying the property for trading purposes. Consequently, the director would not have any property business profit.

Following normal accountancy principles, the company's interest payment on the director's behalf is counted as a business property receipt for the director; however, this is offset by the director's actual obligation to pay the interest.

Warning. If the company doesn't pay rent or interest, the director/shareholder can't secure any income tax relief for the interest.

17.8. THE 10% CGT TAX BREAK

If you dispose of the property used by your company at around the same time as selling your shares in your company, then any gain on that disposal will also qualify for entrepreneur's relief (ER) as an associated disposal, provided certain conditions are met, of course.

TAX BREAK

With ER, your capital gain will be reduced to 5/9ths of the full gain, making your effective Capital Gains Tax (CGT) rate 10% and not 18%; subject to a gains cap of £2 million.

Both conditions that have to be met to qualify for ER as an associated disposal are:

- the property is disposed of as part of your withdrawal from participation in the business carried on by your personal company or the business carried on by your trading group; and
- the property was used for the purposes of the business for a least one year to the date of disposal of the shares, or the date of cessation of the company's business if earlier.

The conditions unfortunately prevent you from selling the property used by your company and getting ER as an associated disposal by selling off a small number of your shares at the same time.

17.8.1. Time limit

The legislation doesn't give a time limit during which an associated disposal must be made. However, the Taxman's guidance says a disposal may be associated if it's:

- within one year of the cessation of business; or

- within three years of the cessation of business and the property hasn't been leased/used for any other purpose at any time after the business ceased; or

- where the business has not ceased, within three years of a material disposal provided the property has not been used for any purpose other than that of the business.

17.8.2. The rent trap

If any of the following apply, the amount of the gain on the associated disposal of the property that would have been subject to ER, is reduced:

- the asset has only been used in the business for part of your period of ownership

- only part of an asset has been used for the purposes of the business

- you were only involved in the business as an employee/officer for part of the time the asset was used for the business

- rent was paid to you for the use of the asset by your personal company in the period after April 5 2008.

17.8.3. Stop charging rent?

Standard practice under the old CGT rules prior to ER was to hold business property outside of the company, and to charge the company a commercial rent for its use. Full business asset taper relief would apply on any gain made on the disposal of the let property and the rent paid was a useful way to extract funds free of NI from the company.

With the abolition of business asset taper relief you must calculate whether the long-term possibility of ER is worth more than the short-term benefit of NI-free rent.

Where a rent has been charged for the use of the property by the company (which will commonly be the case where the property was purchased by the owner raising a mortgage on it) will restrict ER. Even if the rent ceased from April 2008, the period before 2008 will also be taken into account in relation to a material disposal, and thus restrict relief.

The restriction placed on ER is a percentage of market rent charged.

Example

Charles has potential gains on his shares of around £200,000.
His premises are standing at a gain of £500,000 and are likely to be similarly valued at the point of sale. He has charged around 50% of the market rent to cover interest on a loan to purchase the property.

The company pays Corporation Tax at the rate of 21% and the rent charged each year is £10,000.

Loss of tax relief on the rentals costs the company £2,100 per annum. However, to extract £10,000 to pay the interest charge would also cost Charles at least 25% in tax (if taken as a dividend) - taking a gross dividend of £13,333 would put him to £10,000 in funds. So not drawing the rent could cost as much as £2,100 + £3,333 = £5,433 per annum.

Potential loss of ER is currently 50% x £500,000 x 4/9 x 18% = £20,000. Eliminating the rent now would allow a proportion of the gain to attract more CGT. Removing the rent may not be the best option, as it would be impossible to remove all of the impact of the loss of relief, only to reduce it. At a potential cost of £5,433 per annum, this would be unlikely to benefit Charles.

17.8.4. Pre-sale transfer

The key issues you and your advisor will need to take into account when talking about moving the property into the company to avoid the ER rent trap, include:

1. Switching the property into the company before sale will attract Stamp Duty Land Tax (SDLT) on the value of the property. However, it will enable the property to count as part of the material disposal gain when the shares in the company are disposed of.

2. Putting the property into the company would also provide protection for Inheritance Tax purposes, promoting the rate of relief from 50% to 100% as business property.

3. If the property is kept outside the company, a subsequent disposal of the property must take place at a time you sell the remaining shares in the company (or a time when you still hold 5% of the ordinary share capital). It doesn't, however, have to be sold to the purchaser of the shares, and could be sold to an unconnected third party. Any sale at any other time will be fully taxable at 18%.

4. Staying outside the company allows flexibility should the property become surplus to requirements and the owner seeks to let it to a third party. Inside the company there's the tax risk that this would deny ER on the value of the shares as letting the property would be a non-trading activity. This would compromise the trading company status and therefore deny relief on the shares.

5. If you stop paying the rent to increase ER, this may not be the best option, as it would be impossible to remove all of the impact of the loss of relief, only reduce it.

17.9. SELLING YOUR PROPERTY TO YOUR COMPANY

Although a property is personally owned and not exposed to the company's creditors on winding up, in many cases, banks or lenders will secure a charge on the property. Consequently, as far as commercial risk is concerned, there may be little difference whether the property is owned by the company or the shareholder.

TAX BREAK

The sale of the director's personally owned property, such as the trading premises used by the company, generally enables funds to be extracted from the company in a tax and NI-efficient way.

Such a transaction is a disposal for CGT purposes, based on market value of the property, regardless of the actual amount. However, given current property values the gain may not be significant. However, SDLT may be payable on the purchase by the company.

Some care is needed to ensure that the property is not sold at overvalue, since the excess amount could be treated as employment income (or as a shareholder dividend) and taxed at income tax rates (up to 50%) not CGT (18%).

TAX BREAK

An immediate chargeable gain can be avoided by selling the property to the company at its original base cost. Although the disposal will still be worked out by reference to market value, the unrealised element of the gain can be held over.

KEY POINTS

Charging rent
- by paying you rent, the company reduces its taxable profits which in turn reduces the Corporation Tax it pays
- there is no employers' or employees' NI to pay on rents
- you can deduct a wide range of expenses from the rent you receive before it's taxed, as long as they relate to the property
- if the property is owned jointly with your spouse, 50% of the income can be taxed in their name at their own tax rate
- any rent paid to you that is in excess of the market rate for the property, may be taxed as additional salary.

Recovering VAT
- providing the building is used for commercial purposes (not a residential property), you can register for VAT and opt to tax it, which means charging VAT on the rent. However, you are now able recover all the VAT on your costs.

Interest only
- instead of charging a rent, the director could arrange for the company to pay the interest on their personal borrowings that are taken out to purchase or improve the property
- if the company doesn't pay rent or interest, the director-shareholder can't secure any income tax relief for the interest.

Entrepreneurs' relief (ER)
- if you dispose of the property used by your company at around the same time as selling your shares in your company, then any gain on that disposal could also qualify for ER as an associated disposal
- with ER your capital gain will be reduced to 5/9ths of the full gain, making your effective Capital Gains Tax (CGT) rate 10% and not 18%; subject to a gains cap of £2 million
- where a rent has been charged for the use of the property by the company, this will restrict ER. If you stop paying the rent to increase ER this may not be the best option, as it would be impossible to remove all of the impact of the loss of relief.

Selling your property to the company
- the sale of the director's personally owned property (such as the trading premises used by the company) generally enables funds to be extracted from the company in a tax and NI-efficient way

- an immediate chargeable gain can be avoided by selling the property to the company at its original base cost. Although the disposal will still be worked out by reference to market value, the unrealised element of the gain can be held over.

As your company's landlord

CHAPTER 18

Other NI breaks

18.1. INTRODUCTION

Generally, with a limited company if you want to benefit from the profits of the business personally, you have to draw money out. The two chief ways of doing this are drawing a tax-efficient salary as a director or by paying a tax-efficient dividend from the company on your shares.

Other variations of these basic profit extraction methods which can also save on NI include:

- charging your company a royalty or licence fee for using one of your inventions/ ideas
- selling personal assets to your company.

If you still decide to take a significant salary and/or bonus from your company, you'll need to keep an eye on what your total NI bill is likely to be, so as to maximise your after-NI income.

18.2. FORTHCOMING NI HIKES

The good news is that the increase in NI bills for employers and employees don't come into effect until April 6 2011. However, from that date high earners will be dealt a double blow as they will in future pay 12% (currently 11%) on earnings up to £43,888 and 2% (currently 1%) on all earnings above this. Indeed, anyone earning £150,000 or more will find themselves paying more than half their income as tax. Not only are they hit by the 50% income tax, they will then have to pay a further 2% NI.

Your company, as an employer, will be hit even harder. The company pays 12.8% of its workers' salaries as NI. This is to increase to 13.8%. Employers' Class 1A NI on taxable benefits-in-kind is also set to rise to 13.8%.

Per £1,000 of earnings	Cost at 2010/11 rates	Cost at 2011/12 rates
Employees' NI 11%/12%	£110	£120
Employees' NI 1%/2%	£10	£20
Employers' NI 12.8%/13.8%	£128	£138

One strategy for directors would be to look at a salary sacrifice (SS) scheme for 2011/12 purely to negate the increase in NI. In most cases both the director and the company wins. This could be test driven in the current tax year 2010/11 saving NI at current rates, and if successful kept in place for 2011/12 when NI rises.

An SS involves a director giving up part of their salary in exchange for a benefit-in-kind. That might be a taxable benefit-in-kind, such as a car, or a tax-exempt one, such as a mobile phone. Obviously, the latter is preferable as it will save you both tax and NI.

18.2.1. Practical points

1. As a director/employee, sign the SS agreement before the reduced salary takes effect, otherwise the Taxman will ask for tax and NI on the benefit as if it were salary.

2. If your company gives you money to pay for the benefit, the Taxman will treat this as if it were salary. So get your company to pay for the benefit directly, e.g. for a mobile, the contract must be between your company and the phone provider.

3. An SS scheme will only be effective for tax and NI if the benefit is offered to all employees. However, not all employees have to take you up on the offer for the SS to be tax effective for those that do, but the offer must be there.

4. Sign an amendment to your contract of employment.

> **TAX BREAK**
>
> Swap salary for a range of NI-free benefits-in-kind to get around this planned NI hike.

18.3.   ROYALTIES AND LICENCE FEES

> **TAX BREAK**
>
> Royalties and licence fees paid to you are not subject to NI.

If you have a great idea for a new product or process, you could apply for a patent in your own name. The company can then pay you royalty fees for the right to exploit that patent by developing and marketing the product.

Alternatively, you could think up a new design for one of your company's products and register it in your name, with the company paying you a licence fee for using it. Examples are computer programs, manuals or books of any kind, all of which you write in your own time. Licence fees are payments for the use or exploitation of a copyright.

18.3.1. How do you set up this up?

Royalties and licence fees are similar in that they are both payments for the privilege of using some intellectual property that is protected by a patent or copyright. Setting them up, however, does have its differences.

18.3.2. How much can you charge?

A commercial licence is normally granted in return for a percentage of sales, in the range of 5% to 20%. It's important that the Taxman can see that the licence fee has been calculated on a commercial basis and is not a disguised bonus or dividend from the company. So make the fee a percentage of turnover.

As long as the terms of the formal agreement between you and your company are reasonable, the Taxman will not be able to argue that this is disguised remuneration, which would be subject to NI.

18.3.3. Practical points

1. The licence fee must be paid under a legal agreement between you and the company. The fee should be linked to the sales of the product that uses your copyright or patent, so the success of the product is your only restriction on how much is paid. If the fee is a percentage of profits, it looks more like a dividend than a business expense and so the Taxman may not allow you to claim a royalty/licence fee as a tax deduction.

2. The payment of a royalty will reduce the amount of Corporation Tax (CT) paid by the company on its total profits for the year, but it can't be used to turn a profit into a loss or increase tax losses. If the company has no taxable profits, the royalty payment is carried forward to be deducted in the next accounting period. Licence fees paid for the use of copyright material or designs can be deducted from the company's profits to reduce the amount of CT it pays. There is no restriction about losses.

3. If the company pays you a royalty for the use of a patent held in your name, it must deduct basic rate income tax at 20% before it pays the net amount to you. This tax is then paid over to the Taxman. The company should give you a certificate to show how much tax it has deducted from your royalty payments during a tax year. This tax deducted at source will then reduce any additional tax you may have to pay on your income. If the company pays you a licence fee, it's not required to deduct income tax.

4. If you live outside the UK, the company should normally deduct basic rate tax from a licence fee. However, the company does not have to do so if that income is covered by a Double Taxation Agreement between the UK and the country you live in.

18.3.4. Deductible expenses

When you register a patent you must pay an initial fee and each year thereafter keep it in force. The patent fees can be deducted from the income you receive.

A copyright is not granted but arises automatically, so there are no fees to pay unless you register a design. The cost of this can be deducted from your income.

The cost of drawing up a legal agreement between you and the company can also be deducted from the income you receive.

There are no special income tax rates for this type of income. This means that the rate of tax you finally pay depends on your total income during the tax year.

Unless you are normally resident overseas the company should not deduct tax from the licence fee it pays to you for the use of copyright material. This means no tax is paid up-front.

18.3.5. On your tax return

Income earned from patents or copyrights should be shown on your tax return, under "Taxable income not entered elsewhere". You need to enter both the amount you received and any tax deducted by the company.

If you receive payments for the use of copyrights or patents from other sources, then this could be treated as a trade. Income and expenses would then be shown on the "Self-employment" pages of your tax return.

18.4. DIRECTOR SELLS TO COMPANY

TAX BREAK

There is no NI due on this method of extracting profits from your company.

As an individual you can sell an asset such as a building, a vehicle or other goods that you own to the company. However, when you do sell goods or services to the company you should issue an invoice showing the total value of the items or services provided and the VAT due (if any). You can stipulate the terms of payment on the invoice. If the company delays payment beyond the period stated in your terms, you can charge interest on the overdue amount.

When you sell a large capital asset such as a building to the company, the terms of payment will be included within the contract of sale drawn up by your solicitor.

It's possible to leave the amount owing to you for the sale of an asset to the company as a loan from you. The company should credit the amount owing to your director's loan account, and you will be able to draw the money owed when the cash is available. The company can also pay you interest on the outstanding purchase price.

18.4.1. Does it matter what price you charge?

When you sell an asset to your company such as a building, the profit you make will be subject to Capital Gains Tax rather than income tax. The higher the price the company pays for the asset, the greater the gain in your hands and the more tax you will have to pay.

If you own most of the shares in the company so that you control the votes connected with those shares, you and the company are known as connected parties. For tax purposes all transactions between connected parties are deemed to occur at market value even if no money changes hands. You will be taxed on the profit from the sale as if you had received the market value for the asset.

As a director of the company you are also known as a related party. All significant transactions with related parties must be shown in a note to the company's annual accounts. This is where the Taxman will pick them up from to ask the market value question.

18.4.2. Tax return entries

Income. Your income from selling goods or services on a regular basis to the company must be reported on the "Self-employment" pages of your tax return. According to the Taxman when you sell goods or services on a regular basis you are carrying on a trade in your own name and must be treated as a self-employed person.

Trading profits. The rate of income tax that applies to the profits you make when you sell items to the company regularly depends on your total income during the tax year.

Gains. If you sell a capital asset to the company, you must report this on the "Capital Gains" pages of your tax return. However, if all the gains you make total less than £10,100 (for 2009/10 and 2010/11), you do not have to report them. You are also saved the bother of making an entry on these pages if the assets are: **(1)** cars; **(2)** property you occupied within the last three years as your main home; **(3)** government stocks known as gilts; **(4)** foreign currency; or **(5)** moveable possessions (known as chattels) sold for less than £6,000.

If you make a capital gain on selling assets to your company, the tax you pay depends on the level of your other income during the tax year and whether you have any capital losses that can be set against the gain. The remaining gains are first set-against losses made in the same year (or brought forward from earlier years) made on transactions with the same company. The net gains are added to your other income to see what tax band they fall into. The tax rate that applies to gains is currently 18%.

If, for some reason, you generate a loss when selling an asset to your company it can also be recorded on the "Capital Gains" pages. However, you will only able to set that loss against gains between you and your company, which means you can't offset them against, say, investment gains.

18.4.3. Self-employed NI to pay

When you sell an asset to your company there's no NI charge on the capital gain you make. However, if you regularly sell goods or services to the company, you will be treated as operating a trade in your own name. As a self-employed person trading with your company you must register with the Taxman to pay Class 2 NI within three months of the date on which you started your trade. This date will normally be the day when you made your first sale. You pay a flat rate of £2.40 per week if your self-employed profits are likely to amount to more than £5,075 in the tax year. The Class 2 NI must be paid quarterly or four-weekly by direct debit or in satisfaction of a demand from the Taxman.

When you sell goods or services in your own name the profit you make on that trade is subject to an NI charge called Class 4. This is charged at the rate of 8% on profits between £5,715 and £43,875 and 1% on profits made above £43,875. The Class 4 NI must be paid with the income tax due on your self-employed profits, i.e. via your tax return.

18.4.4. Deduct expenses

Trade. Any expenses that are incurred wholly and exclusively for that trade can be deducted from the sales income before you pay tax.

Assets. If you sell an asset to the company, you can deduct its cost from the sale proceeds to calculate the net gain you are taxed on. Any costs for improvements you have made to that asset may also be deducted. In addition, the cost of professional fees you incur in the transaction, such as conveyancing fees, are also deductible.

18.4.5. VAT implications

If you include VAT on your invoice, your company must pay it. If your company is VAT registered, it will then be able to claim it back via its VAT return.

Whether you are required to charge VAT depends on what is sold and the total value of the invoices you issue. VAT is chargeable once your total sales exceed, or are expected to exceed, the current registration limit of £68,000. Of course, before you issue an invoice that includes VAT you must register with the VATman.

You don't have to charge VAT on the sale of a domestic property or sale/lease of a commercial building if it's more than three years old.

Even as a VAT-registered person you don't charge VAT on the sale of a pre-owned car, provided you sell that car for less than you bought it for.

NI hike

- from April 6 2011 high earners will be dealt a double blow as they will in future pay 12% (currently 11%) on earnings up to £43,888 and 2% (currently 1%) on all earnings above this
- look at a salary sacrifice scheme for 2011/12 purely to negate the increase in NI. In most cases both the director and the company wins.

Royalties and licence fees

- the company doesn't have to deduct employees' NI from the licence fee it pays to you, or pay any employers' NI
- if you live in the UK, the company should not deduct tax from a licence fee it pays to you. However, it must deduct tax from any royalty payments
- the licence fee should be related to the sales the company generates by using your copyright material or patented invention. So if the company makes a loss you should still receive the licence fee. Compare this to a dividend that can only be paid if the company makes a profit
- you need to own the patent or copyright personally in order to receive the royalty or licence fee. So if the company initially spends money developing an idea you can't suddenly switch it into your name to generate income from it
- to fully protect the idea you will need to register patents in all countries where the invention or design is likely to be available. You also incur some costs in having a formal legal agreement drafted to cover the conditions under which the licence fee is paid and later renegotiated.

Selling to your company

- when you sell a capital asset to the company, there is no NI to pay on the profits you make on that transaction
- the first £10,100 of capital gains you make on selling an asset to the company is tax-free. There is no tax to pay when you sell an asset that is exempt from Capital Gains Tax to the company, such as a car.

CHAPTER 19

Building up a pension fund

19.1. INTRODUCTION

You can extract profit from your company tax effectively by getting it to pay contributions into a your pension scheme. Pension fund contributions enjoy tax relief at up to 40% (subject to the Taxman's limits). If basic rate tax is 20% and you pay £160 into your pension plan, he will add £40 to your contribution, so the total invested is £200. This is known as basic rate tax relief. If you're a higher rate taxpayer, the payments made into your plan will only be increased by basic rate tax relief, but you will be able to claim higher rate tax relief on your annual self-assessment tax return.

Once the contributions are held within the pension fund they can't be accessed until your 55th birthday. If your intention is to save for your retirement then the fact that you can't access your pension fund before age 55 means that those funds will most probably be used for their intended purpose.

At retirement, up to 25% of your pension fund can be taken as tax-free cash and the remainder must be used to provide you with a retirement income.

If you die before you begin taking the benefits from your pension, the funds will normally be passed to your spouse, or other chosen beneficiary, free of Inheritance Tax.

Most contributions to registered personal pensions made by an individual are paid net of basic rate tax. Deducting basic rate tax has the effect of automatically giving you basic rate tax relief. You don't have to claim this tax relief from the Taxman. The pension company reclaims it.

Tax relief for contributions to a registered pension scheme are generous in that income tax relief is given on the greater of £3,600 (gross or 100% of your taxable earnings). Your taxable earnings broadly include employment income and benefits - dividends and investment income are not included.

19.2. HOW MUCH CAN YOU PUT IN?

There's an annual and a lifetime limit on the pension contributions you can make. An annual contribution has been set at £255,000 (it was £245,000 for 2009/10). If you exceed this, you will be taxed personally on the excess at 40%.

There's also a lifetime limit of £1.8 million on the pension value attracting relief which will be reviewed at five-yearly intervals. Any excess is subject to a recovery charge when you draw benefits from the fund. You'd pay tax at 25% on the excess funds used to create a pension and 40% on those taken as a lump sum.

19.3. FURTHER RULES FOR HIGH EARNERS

Subject to certain exceptions, anyone making a one-off or irregular pension contribution with a relevant income (RI) exceeding £130,000 per year will only get higher rate tax relief on premiums up to a maximum of £20,000 per year.

The problems only start when your RI is greater than £130,000. So one solution is to reduce earnings to below that amount. Even if it's only by £1 it's sufficient to stop the restriction of tax relief being triggered. You can cut your salary to reduce your RI below £130,000 and get your company to pay some or all of this into a pension fund. But this triggers special anti-avoidance rules. The Taxman ignores the salary sacrifice you've made so that your RI isn't treated as reduced. But you can get around this.

The rules only apply where the salary sacrificed is paid into a pension on your behalf. It doesn't affect premiums you pay personally.

So you can get your RI below £130,000 by exchanging salary for a benefit-in-kind worth as much to you but which has a lower value for tax purposes, e.g. a company car. See 12.3 for an example.

Don't just think company cars, consider childcare vouchers, low or interest-free loans, bicycles etc. All of these can be substituted for an equal value salary sacrifice to reduce your RI.

19.4. THE CONTRIBUTION BONUS

Although the flexibility of the pension contribution tax break is significantly limited by the fact that the pension cannot be drawn until the age of 55, this may not matter; a substantial sum invested on your behalf will free up your own savings to be invested in more flexible ways.

Although the company can pay an unlimited contribution into your pension, it will only be able to get tax relief if the contribution passes the "wholly and exclusively" for the business test.

How will the Taxman apply this "wholly and exclusively" test? In the technical pages of his Registered Pension Schemes Manual, he indicates that the contributions paid in respect of a controlling director or members of their family must be in line with that which would have been made to fund the pension provision of an unconnected employee in a similar situation. In other words, it's likely that the Taxman may try to restrict tax relief where substantial contributions are paid in respect of a controlling director or their family.

T<small>IP</small>

Get the company to make a large payment into your pension scheme as a bonus only in years that the company reaches a certain level of profit. This then gives commercial justification for the payment.

T<small>AX BREAK</small>

A company contribution into your pension scheme must be "wholly and exclusively" for the purposes of the trade. You can meet this test by treating it as a "bonus" in high profit years.

Your company's contribution to your pension scheme can be deducted as a trading expense in the period it's paid up to the annual allowance figure (currently £255,000 per year, regardless of your earnings). Any amount the company pays in excess of this is taxed on you.

Unfortunately, the Taxman has said that this test would be judged against the contribution that would have been required to fund the pension provisions for a third party employee in comparable circumstances.

It's difficult to determine such a market rate for a director. In practice, you should be able to claim relief for substantial pension contributions (up to the annual allowance) given that directors invariably carry on considerably more onerous and responsible work than ordinary employees.

However, the Taxman has relaxed his stance somewhat with the following guide to his inspectors: *"Controlling directors are often the driving force behind the company. Where the controlling director is also the person whose work generates the company's income, then the level of the remuneration package is a commercial decision and it is unlikely that there will be a non-business purpose for the level of the remuneration package. It should be noted that remuneration does not include entitlement to dividends etc. arising in the capacity of shareholder."*

Other employees: *"Where the remuneration package paid in respect of other directors (or an employee who is a close relative or friend of the business proprietor or controlling director) is in line with that paid to unconnected employees, you should accept that the package is paid wholly and exclusively for the purposes of the trade."*

19.4.1. Practical points

1. The Taxman might use the wholly and exclusively excuse to disallow a substantial pension contribution. However, inspectors must first clear any proposed company contribution disallowance with the Taxman's Audit and Pension Schemes Services (APSS) first, which should ensure a degree of consistency.

2. As the controlling director you are the driving force behind the company. You are the person whose work generates the company's income. Therefore, the level of your remuneration package (including pension contributions) is a commercial decision and so has a business purpose.

3. A large pension contribution is particularly attractive if you are over 55 years old. Since you can draw funds from your pension scheme (without retiring), you can take a tax-free lump sum equivalent to 25% of the fund and income can be drawn from the fund without NI.

19.5. PENSION FUND INVESTS IN COMPANY

19.5.1. Trading premises

For some time it has been popular for companies to transfer their commercial property into a pension fund for the benefit of its owner-directors. The pension scheme has to pay for the property, which of course it can do out of its accumulated funds, or borrow against the value of the property plus future pension contributions.

In most cases these properties are transferred into the pension fund and then rented back to the company, thereby releasing funds to the company and generating an income stream to the pension fund. A kind of sale and lease back arrangement.

At present it's very tax efficient for a director/shareholder to buy trading premises using a Self-Invested Personal Pension (SIPP). A SIPP is a type of pension scheme which allows you to control the type of investments within your pension fund - you don't have to invest the money with an insurance company.

For example, if a company requires new trading premises the director/shareholder can set up a SIPP to which the company can make pension contributions (depending on the level of the director's earnings). The payments to the pension fund will be deductible for Corporation Tax. Furthermore, the SIPP can buy a property, which it then rents to the company and the rent will also be deductible for Corporation Tax. Because pension funds are exempt from tax, the rent and any future capital gains are not taxable. Inevitably, a number of restrictions apply to such a favourable system. One of these restrictions relates to borrowing.

A SIPP which wishes to buy a property is allowed to borrow up to 50% of the value of the pension fund. So for a property costing £300,000 you would need a pension fund of £200,000, which allows you to borrow the balance of the purchase price of £100,000 (50% of £200,000). That's two-thirds pension fund and one-third borrowing.

To work out the value of the pension fund you'd need under the new rules, here's a handy formula: *Cost of property/1.5 = value the fund needed*. This means that you may have to wait until you have paid substantially more pension contributions into your pension fund before you can afford to buy the trading premises you want.

TAX BREAK

There are tax advantages to using a SIPP. However, to buy the property you want you will have to pay in more by way of pension contributions.

19.5.2. Equipment used in the business

Let's say your company wants to buy a substantial piece of equipment. However, doing so would mean it couldn't also afford this year's contribution to the pension fund. There is, however, a way to do both and get a 200% tax deduction into the bargain.

A small self-administered pension scheme (SSAS), far from being just a piggy bank for retirement, can be used as a tax-free haven here and now. You start with two simple rules of thumb.

Contributions. Any contribution to an SSAS gets tax relief against your company's profits. It doesn't matter how big the contribution is (providing it doesn't over fund the scheme) - unlike director's remuneration which the Taxman can (and does) argue should not be allowed if it's too big.

Loans. The SSAS can lend some of this money back to the company. What it can't do is lend money to you directly as a member of the pension fund. Loans must be secured, not exceed five years (but can be rolled over once) and must be on commercial terms (with equal annual payments and a interest charge at least equal to bank base rate plus 1%). Further, such loans must not exceed 50% of the fund.

What if you can't afford to make both a contribution into your scheme and buy some equipment for the business? Instead of claiming depreciation on some types of asset, like plant and machinery and industrial buildings, the tax rules give your company a special kind of allowance, known as capital allowances. Small companies buying plant and equipment can claim 100% of the cost in the first year of purchase up to £100,000. But there is a way to turn this 100% into 200%.

Step 1. Put the money you were going to use to buy the asset into the SSAS as a contribution. This is 100% tax deductible. It doesn't matter if you have to borrow this money from the bank the scheme still works.

Step 2. The SSAS immediately lends the full amount back to the company and enters into a loan arrangement whereby the SSAS charges the company a commercial interest rate.

Step 3. The company, which has now got its own money back as a loan, uses the money to purchase the asset, on which it claims 100% of the cost by way of capital allowances.

By sending the money around in a circle this way, you've actually got tax relief for it twice, i.e. you have 200% tax relief, all in the same year. First, as a pension contribution, and then as capital allowances on purchased equipment.

Of course with all such ideas, one has to be careful to ensure that you are not seen to be simply using the SSAS as a vehicle for a tax avoidance scheme. So always document the financial reasons why this arrangement came into being.

TAX BREAK

Put the money you were going to use to buy the asset into the SSAS as a contribution. The SSAS lends the full amount back to the company to purchase the asset. Both contribution and purchase are tax deductible.

How much can you put in?

- most contributions to registered personal pensions made by an individual are paid net of basic rate tax. Deducting basic rate tax has the effect of automatically giving you basic rate tax relief

- if you pay higher rate tax on any of your income, you are entitled to higher rate tax relief on personal pension payments but you have to claim it

- because of the high limits for tax relief on pension contributions, it's no longer necessary to maximise your payments each tax year. However, making pension payments up to the amount of your income subject to higher rate tax in any tax year will maximise the tax you can avoid.

Rules for high earners

- it's worth considering making a pension contribution to get a tax break. However, with the many changes to pension tax legislation over the last few years, great care should be taken, as higher rate relief may not be available.

Tax deduction for your company

- a company contribution into your pension scheme must be "wholly and exclusively" for the purposes of the trade. You can meet this test by treating it as a "bonus" in high profit years

- as the controlling director you are the driving force behind the company. Therefore, the level of your remuneration package (including pension contributions) is a commercial decision and so has a business purpose.

Fund invests in company

- there are tax advantages to having your own a Self-Invested Personal Pension scheme which the company pays into. However, to buy a property you want, you will have to pay in more by way of pension contributions

- instead of buying equipment directly, put the money you were going to use to buy the asset into a small self-administered pension scheme as a contribution. The SSAS lends the full amount back to the company to purchase the asset. Both contribution and purchase are then tax deductible.

CHAPTER 20

Restructuring shares

20.1. INTRODUCTION

Developments in the life of your company may make it necessary to change its share structure to help deal with:

- including new shareholders or increasing or decreasing the number of shares in existence

- giving shares to the next generation as part of succession or Inheritance Tax (IHT) planning

- providing a key or new manager with shares as an incentive and to foster loyalty.

20.2. ACQUIRING MORE SHARES

Selling shares in your company is one way of raising long-term finance for your business. This is also known as equity finance. The advantage is that you don't always have to repay the finance or pay interest as you would with an overdraft or bank loan.

Generally, when you buy more shares in the company, this entitles you to more dividends. In fact, a company can have many different types of share that come with different conditions and rights. There are four main types:

- **Ordinary shares.** These are standard shares with no special rights or restrictions. They have the potential to give the highest financial gains, but also have the highest risk. Ordinary shareholders are the last to be paid if the company is wound up. The company may divide them into classes of different values.

- **Preference shares.** These typically carry a right that gives the holder preferential treatment when annual dividends are distributed to shareholders. Shares in this category have a fixed value, which means that you (as such a shareholder) would not benefit from an increase in the company's profits. However, usually you have rights to your dividend ahead of ordinary shareholders if the business is in trouble. Also, where a business is wound up, you are likely to be repaid the nominal value of shares ahead of ordinary shareholders.

- **Cumulative preference shares.** These confer the right for dividends to be carried forward if they can't be paid one year. Dividends on cumulative preference shares must be paid, regardless of the profits of the business.

- **Redeemable shares.** These come with an agreement that the company can buy them back at a future date - this can be at a fixed date or at the choice of the business. A company can't issue only redeemable shares.

Private companies are not permitted to offer or allot their shares to the public. The directors have the power to issue shares up to the amount of the authorised share capital. If further shares are required, the authorised share capital can be increased by a resolution of the existing shareholders.

Where shares are being issued for cash under company law they must first be offered to existing shareholders in proportion to their existing shareholding - generally referred to as pre-emption rights. The offer to existing shareholders remains open for 21 days and the shares can only be taken up elsewhere if a shareholder declines to take up their offer. It's possible to override these statutory pre-emption rights. Some company's articles of association may exclude statutory pre-emption rights, but will usually contain further pre-emption rules. It's always necessary to check the company's articles before a new issue is made.

20.2.1. Loans to acquire shares

The rules for income tax relief on loan interest to buy ordinary shares are basically the same as where borrowings are used to pass funds to a company.

TAX BREAK

In contrast to relief for shareholder loans, the legislation does not require the proceeds received on the share issues to be applied for the purposes of the company's trade. Indeed, interest relief is available where the shares are acquired by subscription or acquired from a third party.

20.3. TRANSFERRING SHARES

Shares in a listed company are transferred through brokers using the Stock Exchange system. However, in a private or unlimited company, shares are usually transferred by private agreement between the seller and buyer, subject to the company's rules and approval of the directors.

Certain taxes apply when you transfer or sell shares:

- if you are transferring shares yourself using a paper stock transfer form, Stamp Duty may be payable when the value is over certain limits. Stamp Duty reserve tax is normally payable when you transfer shares through a broker using the Euroclear service

- any gains you have made on selling shares may be subject to Capital Gains Tax.

If you buy stocks and shares for more than £1,000, you have to pay Stamp Duty. This means you have to send the Taxman a stock transfer form for stamping, along with your payment.

The amount of Stamp Duty you pay is based on the "consideration" you give for the stocks or shares. You pay Stamp Duty at the rate of 0.5% of the value of the consideration, rounded up to the nearest £5, on each document to be stamped.

Example

Alan buys shares using a stock transfer form. He pays £2,500. The Stamp Duty rate is 0.5%. So £2,500 × 0.5% = £12.50. This is rounded up to the nearest £5, which means Alan pays £15 Stamp Duty.

TAX BREAK

If you buy stocks and shares for £1,000 or less, you don't normally have to pay any Stamp Duty. You also don't have to tell the Taxman about the transaction.

All you need to do is:

- make sure the exemption certificate on the back of the stock transfer form has been completed
- send the stock transfer form and the share certificate to your company and they will then issue you with your own share certificate.

20.4. SHARES TO SPOUSE

TAX BREAK

If you transfer shares to your spouse, no CGT liability will arise. And they automatically inherit your base cost and period of ownership of the shares. The taper relief status of the shareholding prior to the transfer is ignored.

20.4.1. When would this be useful?

In order to take best advantage of being taxed separately it may be sensible for property (including shares in your company) to be transferred from you to your spouse or vice versa. Any such transfers are fully effective for tax purposes providing the transfer is an outright gift with no question of transferring to the spouse controlling it or deriving benefit from it and provided the gift is not just a right to income.

Such transfers will be beneficial where your spouse would otherwise waste their personal allowance or where you would be paying higher rate tax while your spouse did not fully use the basic rate band. Make sure you have evidence of the transfers in proper legal form.

20.4.2. When it comes to selling the company

ER trick. If your spouse does not qualify for entrepreneurs' relief (ER), it's possible to use the above rule to improve your overall ER position. This can be done by switching the ownership of the shares (well) before the final disposal into the hands of the spouse with the most favourable ER profile.

Example

Mr Rann has owned 60% of Strong-arm Ltd's ordinary share capital since 2000. His wife has held 20% of Strong-arm Ltd for the same period but has never worked for the company. In May 2010 one of the company's competitors, Softly Softly Ltd, expressed an interest in acquiring Strong-arm Limited. Following advice Mrs Rann decided to transfer her 20% holding to her husband. This enabled Mr Rann to claim full ER on his (then) 80% shareholding in the company. Mrs Rann's shares (which are treated as having been owned by Mr Rann since his wife acquired them can effectively piggyback the business asset status of Mr Rann's 60% holding.

On the other hand, if Mrs Rann retained and sold her 20% holding, her ER would be diluted.

20.5. SHARES TO OTHER FAMILY MEMBERS

Developments in the life of a company may make it necessary to change its structure by including new shareholders. For example, an existing shareholder may wish to give shares to the next generation as part of Inheritance Tax (IHT) planning. If you want to give an asset such as shares to a family member other than your spouse, the Taxman will treat the gift as a disposal at market value for Capital Gains Tax (CGT), i.e. you will pay tax on the difference between the value and the original cost of the shares. This means tax to pay on proceeds you haven't got.

TAX BREAK

However, you can claim to defer (holdover) gains on assets that qualify as business assets, for example shares in an unquoted trading company (s.165 of the **Taxes of Capital Gains Act 1992**). As far as trading companies are concerned the amount of holdover relief on its shares is restricted to the chargeable business assets in its balance sheet.

A transfer of unquoted shares in a trading company will normally be eligible for business asset holdover relief for CGT purposes. This has the effect of eliminating your chargeable gain. The gain is deducted from the transferee's deemed acquisition cost (market value). The held over gain only becomes chargeable if the transferee subsequently makes a disposal of the gifted shares. However, 80% of your company activities must be trading for holdover relief to apply.

Example

On September 18 2010, Chris gives to his son Luke, 30% of the shares in the family company, Pollinations Fruit Importers Ltd, which he incorporated in 1996. The value of the shares transferred has been agreed with the Taxman's Shares Valuation section at £60,000.

CHRIS'S **CGT** CALCULATION	£
Consideration = market value	*60,000*
Less cost of shares disposed of	*(2,500)*
Gain	*57,500*
Less business asset holdover relief	*(57,500)*
Chargeable gain	*Nil*

Luke's base cost will be £2,500 (i.e. the market value of £60,000 less gain held over of £57,500). This is effectively the "cost" of the shares transferred.

A deemed market value disposal also arises where you gift your shares or transfer them at undervalue to another director or an employee in recognition of their services provided to the company.

20.5.1. Joint election

In most cases the Taxman will permit a holdover claim to be made without the need to agree a formal valuation of the gifted shares. This helpful concessionary treatment must be claimed in writing on Form IR295. The transferor and the transferee must jointly elect for holdover relief, except where the transfer is made to trustees in which case only the transferor makes the claim. Both parties must confirm that they are satisfied that the (estimated) value of the shares exceeds its original base cost.

Practical point. Under self-assessment, the holdover election must be made on the prescribed form on helpsheet IR 295, which should preferably be submitted with the transferor's tax return. However, the claim can be submitted separately within the next five years.

20.5.2. Investments

For holdover relief to apply, the shares in question must be unquoted in a trading company or holding company within a trading group.

51% test. Where shares in an investment company are gifted, holdover relief can't be claimed and therefore you will suffer a CGT liability. At the moment, a company's activities must be "wholly or mainly" trading in order to qualify as a trading company, so that the 51% trading test could apply.

80% test. However, the Taxman considers an 80% test more appropriate, although it remains to be confirmed in each case what it's 80% of! Is it 80% of the balance sheet, profits, turnover or something else?

Practical point. If you intend to use holdover relief, check to see what percentage of your investments form your company's balance sheet, profits, turnover etc. Any one of these could be used by the Taxman to look at the "wholly or mainly" trading question.

20.5.3. Other taxes

The transfer of shares by an existing shareholder could qualify as a potentially exempt transfer (PET) for IHT purposes. No IHT liability would therefore arise provided the transferor shareholder survives for seven years. This is subject to transfer of value provisions.

TAX BREAK

The gift of shares qualifies as a PET for IHT purposes. So IHT is avoided if you survive the gift by seven years.

20.6. SHARE BUY-IN

A company has the power to buy back its own shares (a share buy-in) from its shareholders, allowing you to cash in on your shares tax effectively. There would be a tax bill to pay on the difference between the subscription price of the shares and their market value (one of the Taxman's conditions).

A share buy-in can be a very useful device. It's often used to buy out one or more shareholders, using funds within the company (hence avoiding the need to draw funds out and pay income tax on that).

Provided you have held the shares for at least five years you are able to choose between Capital Gains Tax (CGT) or an income distribution (i.e. dividend) treatment.

You would want CGT treatment if you can benefit from substantial ER relief, securing an effective CGT rate of (at least) 10%, compared to an effective rate of tax of 25% for an income distribution. CGT treatment is mandatory if certain conditions are met.

Since a shareholder makes a disposal of shares, this might at first appear to be a capital transaction, however the default position for a purchase of own shares is for it to be taxed as a distribution (i.e. a dividend). For a higher rate taxpayer, this of course means an effective 25% tax rate.

TAX BREAK

It's possible to escape the dividend treatment and secure a capital treatment (and a tax rate of 18%) for a share buy-in, but this requires a close adherence to the rules. Basically, it's necessary to satisfy a number of detailed conditions, which are discussed in more detail below. You have to satisfy all the conditions; failure to meet a single one will cause the transaction to become a distribution and chargeable to income tax.

If a purchase of own shares does qualify for capital treatment, then the capital gain is computed in the usual manner; there are no "special" rules. The amount that the company pays out is brought into the computation of the gain as proceeds and the base cost of the shares set off in the usual way.

20.6.1. Nature of the company

The company making the purchase must be an unquoted trading company, or the unquoted holding company of a trading group. For these purposes a company that deals in shares, securities, land or futures is excluded from the definition of a trading company (despite the fact that these activities may amount to trading for other tax definitions).

20.6.2. Reason for purchase

The purchase of own shares must be for a permissible reason. The transaction must be for the purpose of the trade, and not for the avoidance of tax for enabling the owner of the shares to participate in the company's profits without receiving a dividend.

TAX BREAK

Director/shareholders in trading companies may be able to benefit from entrepreneur's relief (ER) on the buy-in.

What is likely to be accepted by the Taxman as for the purpose of the trade? You might be concerned that any transactions at shareholder level would not generally be held to be anything to do with the trade of the company. Fortunately, in practice, it's not quite as restrictive as that. Indeed, guidance issued by the Taxman allows a share buy-in if:

- there's a disagreement between shareholders over the management of the company and the disagreement is having or is expected to have an adverse effect on the company's trade, and the effect of the transaction is to remove the dissenting shareholder entirely

- the purpose is to ensure an "unwilling shareholder" who wishes to end their association with the company does not sell their shares to someone who might not be acceptable to the other shareholders.

Circumstances with "unwilling shareholders" are quite common and include:

- an outside shareholder who has provided equity finance (whether or not with the expectation of redemption or sale to the company) and who now wishes to withdraw finance

- a controlling shareholder who is retiring as a director and wishes to make way for new management

- personal representatives of a deceased shareholder, where they wish to realise the value of their shares

- a legatee of a deceased shareholder, who does not wish to hold shares in the company.

Trap. The Taxman will not, however, accept a purchase of own shares if it basically appears to be a mechanism for extracting profits from the company whilst the director/shareholder continues their involvement (e.g. a directorship or an appointment as a consultant).

To this end they will expect the shareholder to completely terminate their involvement with the company and give up the entire shareholding (although keeping back a shareholding of 5% for sentimental reasons is permitted).

It's in the nature of such tests that there will always be some cases where there is doubt as to whether conditions are satisfied or not. Fortunately, the Taxman operates a statutory clearance procedure about the transaction.

Unless the sums involved are relatively trivial, it's generally recognised as best practice for your tax advisor to make a clearance application to confirm whether the transaction will be accepted as benefit of the trade, and not for the avoidance of tax, before it takes place.

20.6.3. Residence

The person selling the shares must be UK resident and ordinarily resident for tax purposes throughout the year in which the purchase takes place.

That said, a person who is non-resident will probably prefer the buy-in to be treated as income in any event, since they will have no higher rate tax liability on the resulting distribution.

Warning. Don't affect a purchase of own shares hoping to benefit from CGT treatment and leave the UK later in the same tax year.

20.6.4. Holding period

It's necessary to have held shares for at least five years. The planning point here is to be wary about moving shares of trading companies around unnecessarily lest it prejudice the ability to get capital treatment on purchase of own shares. Indeed, business holdover relief makes it deceptively easy to do this and it might be advantageous to move shares around to increase entitlement to entrepreneurs' relief. Neither of these points can alter the position with regard to the five-year period for share buy-ins.

On the other hand, ownership by your spouse or civil partner is included in the five-year period.

20.6.5. Substantial reduction

It's necessary to ensure that the total nominal value that the vendor owns immediately after the purchase (expressed as a fraction of the total share capital) does not exceed 75% of the corresponding fraction before the purchase. The holding of associates is taken into account for this test.

For these purposes an associate is:

- a spouse or civil partner

- a minor child (or parent of that minor child)

- a person connected with a company and any company controlled by it

- where the person connected with a company controls another company. The latter company in relation to the first company

- for shares held by trustees, any person who provided property to trustees, any associate of that person or any person who is or may become beneficially entitled to a significant interest in the shares (an interest of over 5% of value of settled property).

The test can be a deceptive one and passing it is not the same thing as needing to sell at least 25% of your holding.

Example

The total share capital of Border Ltd (an unquoted trading company) is 100,000 ordinary shares. Alan owns 10,000 ordinary shares. The remaining 90,000 shares in Border Ltd are held by unrelated parties. A share buy-in takes place and 2,500 of Alan's shares are acquired. This mean's Alan's shareholding reduces to 7,500 shares and Border Ltd will have a total share capital of 97,500 shares.

Fraction before purchase 10,000/100,000 = 0.100. Fraction after purchase 7,500/97,500 = 0.077

The fraction after purchase exceeds 75% of the fraction before the purchase. Consequently, Alan fails the substantial reduction test.

However, suppose Alan sells 2,703 shares, then his holding would become 7,297 shares. Moreover, Border Ltd would have a total issued capital of 97,297. This means the calculation would now run as follows: Fraction before purchase 10,000/100,000 = 0.100. Fraction after purchase 7,207/97,297 = 0.075. The fraction after purchase now does not exceed 75%. As a consequence, Alan passes the substantial reduction test.

In practice, given the need to reduce a holding completely in order to satisfy the benefit of trade test, this requirement may be redundant.

However, it may be possible to persuade the Taxman that the exit can be achieved over a period of time in order for it to qualify as being for the benefit of the trade, which means that care must be taken how instalments are structured.

20.6.6. No connection

The Taxman will not permit the shareholder whose shares are acquired to have any connection with the company after the buy-in has taken place. Whilst in other tax contexts connection means control over 50%, for these purposes a 30% test is used. This is applied to the following: issued ordinary share capital; loan capital and issued share capital; voting power and assets available to equity shareholders.

In applying the test he looks at both the shareholder and other persons who themselves are connected to the shareholder, such as trustees and older relatives. Adult children are not included, though.

A share buy-in can be used to acquire the shares of the parents of a family trading company and get capital treatment, leaving the company in the hands of the next generation, so long as they have achieved the age of majority.

The test also takes loans into account. This includes loans of the proceeds of the buy-in. This applies even if paying consideration for the shares over time is purely a commercial arrangement, say, because the company's cash flow can't support anything else.

Example

Chappell Ltd has an issued share capital of £100 (made up of £1 shares) and a balance on its profit and loss reserve is £3m. Ian owns 20% of the ordinary share capital of the company and it is agreed that the company will undertake a purchase of own shares to buy Ian's holding. The agreed price is £1.4m.

Chappell Ltd can't afford to pay entire the £1.4m all at once and so it's agreed that Ian will lend £300,000 back to the company immediately after the purchase and his loan balance will be repaid over a period of time, as and when the company's resources allow. Ian is entirely unconnected with any of the other shareholders.

If the transaction proceeds in this manner, Ian's interest in the company's loan capital plus share capital of the company will be:

	TOTAL (£)	IAN'S INTEREST (£)
Share capital	80	0
Loan capital	300,000	300,000
	300,080	300,000

Ian's interest in the company is therefore: 300,000/300,080 = 99.97%. The connection test has therefore failed.

There are, however, ways to plan around this. One method is for the company to undertake a bonus issue of shares, so as to swap the loan balance and push it below the 30% threshold.

Suppose Chappell Ltd does undertake a bonus issue and issues £1,250,000 of new share capital. Its total share capital becomes £1,250,100. Ian participates in this bonus issue and his shareholding becomes:

	SHARES
Original holding	20
20% share of bonus issues (£1,250,000 x 20%)	250,000
	250,020

The share buy-in will reduce the company's total issued share capital to £1,000,080 (being £1,250,100 less £250,020). Now the position after the buy-in and loan-back will become:

	TOTAL (£)	IAN'S INTEREST (£)
Share capital	1,000,080	0
Loan capital	300,000	300,000
	1,300,080	300,000

Ian's interest is now: 300,000/1,300,080 = 23.08%. Accordingly, Ian has passed the connection test. However, Chappell Ltd's reserves have been reduced thus:

	£
Reserves before transaction	3,000,000
Applied to bonus issue	(1,250,000)
Used for share buy-in	(1,400,000)
Remaining reserves	350,000

Chappell Ltd has had its reserves depleted by far more than the amount it has paid to Ian. This will restrict its ability to pay future dividends to the remaining shareholders.

However, this does need distributable reserves. Depending on how much is lent back, this might well require reserves in excess of what is to be paid out by means of the share buy-in.

Even if such reserves are available, it has the effect of eliminating them so they can no longer be used to fund future dividends or indeed purchase own shares.

It is significant to note that the Taxman has confirmed that both a loan-back and the bonus issue to ensure the connection test can be met are acceptable planning.

Another approach might be to buy all the shares at once and set completion of that contract to take place on defined dates, provided sufficient distributable reserves exist at those dates.

The documentation does need to be drawn up carefully and it can lead to legal complications, particularly if the requisite reserves cease to exist, say, because of trading losses, before the contract can be completed.

Previous bonus issues. If the company has made a previous bonus issue, any subsequent purchase of own shares will automatically be treated as a distribution, regardless of whether it can satisfy the above tests or not.

TIP

Before planning any purchase of own shares investigate the share history of the company to identify any bonus issues that might have taken place over the years.

By the same token, if a bonus issue is going to be used to facilitate a loan-back in the manner described above, keep an eye on the possibility of a subsequent purchase of own shares taking place.

20.7. FUNDING A SHARE BUY-IN

Let's say your company agrees to buy-in the shares in successive stages conditional upon future distributable profits/cash flow being available. However, any plan must pass the substantial reduction test. This means that after each tranche of shares are bought back, your remaining interest in the company must not exceed 75% of your original interest (the repurchased shares are immediately cancelled).

Trap. In determining your interest in the company the Taxman can include the shareholding etc. of your associates. For example, a husband and wife are associated persons and their shares must be combined when determining whether the interest in the company has been reduced.

TIP

To fund a buy-back, issue new redeemable shares. Avoid the substantial reduction problem by making sure the redeemable (preference) shares are issued to someone who is not associated with you for CGT purposes.

TIP

Get advanced clearance from the Taxman for the whole plan. And make sure you stick exactly to what you have told him in the clearance procedure.

TAX BREAK

Use a share buy-back to extract profits from your company. Fund this with an issue of redeemable preference shares to a new shareholder. They can be your son or daughter provided they are over 18.

Acquiring more shares

- the rules for income tax relief on loan interest to buy ordinary shares are basically the same as where borrowings are used to pass funds to a company. However, in contrast to relief for shareholder loans, the legislation does not require the proceeds received on the share issues to be applied for the purposes of the company's trade. Indeed interest relief is available where the shares are acquired by subscription or acquired from a third party.

Transferring shares

- your company can normally be partitioned (without extra tax cost) amongst different shareholders and different types of share
- it may be sensible for shares in your company to be transferred from you to your spouse and vice versa. This will be beneficial where your spouse would otherwise waste their personal allowance or where you would be paying higher rate tax while they aren't fully utilising the basic rate band
- if you transfer shares to your spouse, no CGT liability will arise. They automatically inherit your base cost and the period of ownership of the shares. The entrepreneurs' relief status of the shareholding prior to the transfer is ignored
- a gift of shares by you to another family member represents a disposal at market value as far as the Taxman is concerned. However, both parties can elect to hold over the gain. The effect of the holdover election is to pass the contingent liability to the new shareholder(s), which only materialises when they dispose of the shares.

Share buy-in

- funds can be extracted from your company in a CGT-efficient manner by arranging a share buy-in. However, you have to demonstrate that this is motivated by ongoing benefits to the trade of your company. CGT treatment of a share buy-in is generally only available where the shares have been held for five years.

CHAPTER 21

Inheritance Tax breaks

21.1. INTRODUCTION

It's important to provide for the continuity of your business and its management in the event of your death, disability or predetermined retirement plans. The current tax regime is probably as favourable as it is ever going to be in terms of providing for succession in the family or owner-managed company. For example, all shareholdings in unquoted trading companies are completely exempt from IHT.

21.2. KEEPING BELOW THE IHT THRESHOLD

Inheritance Tax (IHT) is based on the death value of your estate when it passes to people other than your spouse or a charity. The tax may also be levied on lifetime transfers either immediately, or if you die within seven years of the transfer. If you are domiciled in the UK, then your worldwide property will be subject to IHT. If you are not UK domiciled, then only your UK property will be liable.

The first £325,000 of a person's estate is known as the IHT nil-rate band (NRB) because the rate of IHT charges on this amount is 0%, so is free of tax. IHT at the rate of 40% is only paid if the taxable value of an estate is over this amount.

Example

ASSETS AND LIABILITIES	£
Value of family home	270,000
Mortgage	(50,000)
Shares	35,000
Building society accounts and ISAs	40,000
Chattels	25,000
Life assurance claims	100,000
Total	390,000
NRB	325,000
Taxable at 40%	95,000
Tax due	38,000
Net estate	57,000

21.2.1. The seven-year rule

If you make a gift which is known as a potentially exempt transfer (PET), as long as you live seven years, it will be completely free of tax. However, if you die within the seven-year period, it will fall into charge with the rest of your chargeable estate. Fortunately, there is taper relief. If you die between years three and seven, the tax payable will be reduced by 20% increments down to zero. So it makes sense to make gifts as soon as you practically can in order to get the seven-year clock running.

21.2.2. Gifts with reservation

The Taxman isn't stupid and won't let you give things away but still keep them. For example, if you have a collection of old masters on your walls, and you simply say to your children "they're yours", and leave them on your walls. The gift won't count. The rule is that when you give something away, you must exclude yourself from benefiting.

21.2.3. Keeping value outside the estate

One of the main considerations is to keep your assets outside of your taxable estate. For example, you can have all your life assurance policies written into trust so they do not form part of your estate when you die, and simply pass straight to your chosen beneficiaries without probate delay or IHT.

21.2.4. Skipping a generation

This may appear to be mean, but it's actually very good planning.

Imagine that the grandparents have wealth they wish to dispose of. The natural inclination is to pass on to their children. However, the children might well be middle aged and facing IHT problems of their own. It just makes no sense to increase their estates. The grandparents should therefore consider giving the money directly to the grandchildren, in trust if necessary, so that tax is never levied on that money in either generation.

> *Example*
>
> *If the grandparents leave £250,000 to the middle generation, the tax is £40,000. The net £210,000 seven years later may have grown to £500,000. If the middle generation then dies, then this might well be taxed at 40% leaving a net amount of £240,000 for the grandchildren. Had the £210,000 gone directly to them, and then all things being equal, they would now have the full £400,000 in their estate, so that £160,000 would be saved.*

21.2.5. Tax breaks for gifts

There are tax breaks for gifts and transfers you can make each tax year, which enable you to avoid IHT altogether. These are as follows.

£3,000 annual exemption. Each individual may give £3,000 away every year without any IHT consequence at all. If you did not use this last year, then you may carry it forward and give away £6,000 this year. So a husband and wife can give £12,000 away, thus saving £4,800 (£12,000 x 40%) in potential tax without any difficulty at all.

£250 gifts. Gifts of up to £250 may be given to anybody at all. They are unlimited and you could, theoretically, give £250 to every teacher in your children's school. However, curiously enough, if you give £251 to anybody, the whole £251 will be taxable and not just the odd £1.

Gifts on marriage. You are able to make gifts to one of the partners of a marriage or their children. The limits are £5,000 if the donor is a parent of one of the individuals getting married, or £2,500 if the donor is a grandparent or great-grandparent. Otherwise, the limit for tax-free gifts is £1,000.

Normal expenditure out of income. You can give away almost any amount as long as it's seen to be normal expenditure from your income, is not manifestly from capital, and is capable of being repeated year on year. So if you are retired with a fantastic index-linked pension of, say, £50,000 p.a. and only spend £10,000 a year, you could theoretically give the rest away as normal expenditure without IHT consequences.

21.2.6. Pre-owned assets tax

An income tax charge on certain pre-owned assets (POAs) may be levied on you. The POA legislation is primarily aimed at a number of IHT-avoidance arrangements that broadly enable you to dispose of your assets (for IHT purposes) whilst retaining the ability to use or have access to them. Such arrangements would generally be structured to avoid gift with reservation of benefit rules. However, given its wide ranging nature, the POA legislation could also affect many innocent transactions sometimes in an unsuspected manner.

Example

In January 2009, Peter gifted shares worth around £70,000 in People Management Ltd to his son Paul. In May 2013 these shares are sold for some £100,000. His son uses the proceeds towards the purchase of a small bungalow in Cornwall for £150,000 which is occupied by Peter as his main residence on a rent-free basis. The annual rental value of the bungalow in 2013/4 is £15,000.

In this case the shares are "other property" under the POA rules that were sold by Peter with the proceeds being used to buy an interest in land (the bungalow) to be occupied by his father.

Peter will have an annual POA taxable figure of £10,000. This is calculated as £15,000 x (£100,000/£150,000) = £10,000.

The key exemption from the POA charge is if the total taxable amount for the tax year does not exceed £5,000. **Note.** This is not an exempt band so that annual rental value of say £5,100 would be fully chargeable to POA.

Similar rules apply if you benefit from having free or low cost enjoyment of chattels (such as valuable paintings or ornaments that you formerly owned). The calculation of the POA charge for chattels is slightly different in that the official rate of interest (currently 4.25%) is applied to their rental value.

TAX BREAK

Any amount you pay for the use or enjoyment of your chattels is deducted in arriving at the taxable amount.

21.3. TWO NIL-RATE BANDS FOR SPOUSES

Where assets are transferred between spouses, they are exempt from IHT. This can mean that if, on the death of your spouse, they leave all their assets to you, the benefit of the NRB to pass on assets tax-free to other members of the family, normally the children, is not used.

TAX BREAK

Where one spouse dies and does not use their NRB to make tax-free bequests to other members of the family, the unused amount can be transferred and used by the second spouse's estate on their death.

In effect, you and your spouse now have an NRB that is worth up to double the amount.

Example

If on the death of the first spouse, they leave legacies of £70,000 to each of the two children, the total of £140,000 would be a chargeable transfer for IHT. But because it's below £325,000, the legacies pass free of tax and £185,000 (or 57%) of the NRB is unused. The unused amount can be transferred to the second spouse. If, when they die the IHT NRB is, say, £325,000, they will be entitled to use this plus 60% of this amount again. This represents the 57% unused element of the spouse that dies first.

21.4. BUSINESS PROPERTY RELIEF

100% business property relief (BPR) has applied to **all** shareholdings (including non-voting and preference shares) in unquoted trading companies. (Shares in AIM companies are unquoted for this purpose and hence rank for 100% BPR.) Unquoted shares are completely exempt from IHT both on lifetime transfers and on death. BPR works by reducing the value transferred, in this case to nil.

To qualify for BPR you need to have held your shareholding for at least two years prior to the transfer/death. BPR is available for both working and passive shareholders; it's not necessary for the shareholder to be a director or work full-time.

21.4.1. Avoiding the investment tag

Your shares will not qualify for BPR if your company's business consists wholly or mainly in the dealing of securities, stocks and shares or land and buildings. Indeed, BPR is denied if your company wholly or mainly makes investments.

Problems can arise in practice if your company carries on qualifying and non-qualifying activities, for example a company which builds houses (qualifying) but also receives rental income on a number of properties (non-qualifying). The Taxman's current approach is to look at your company's turnover, profit and underlying asset values for each activity to determine what it "mainly" does. Mainly is interpreted for this purpose as being over 50%. If the predominant activity is qualifying, then BPR is given on the entire value of the company's shares. Where it's non-qualifying (for example property letting) no BPR is given. It's an all or nothing test.

21.4.2. Excepted assets tax break

The Taxman can also reduce/restrict the BPR on your company shares if the company has "excepted" assets in its balance sheet. An asset is excepted if it's not used wholly or mainly for business purposes unless it's required for future use in the business. The Taxman applies the excepted asset rules to investments, let property and substantial cash balances.

The restriction works by excluding part of the value transferred. For example, only £150,000 of a cash balance of £450,000 was held to be required for future use in the business so that the remaining £300,000 constituted an excepted asset. This is still very much a question of negotiation and would, for example, depend on whether your shares were valued based on earnings or assets.

Your trading company will qualify for BPR even if it also has a small investment business. This is on the basis that your company's business is not wholly and mainly the making or holding of investments.

21.4.3. 50% for business premises

It's not uncommon for the company's trading property to be owned by you and let to your company. Property let to the company for trading purposes will generally qualify for the higher rate of business asset taper relief for CGT purposes on a subsequent sale. However, this ownership outside the company is detrimental for IHT purposes.

BPR of 50% is available on land, buildings, machinery or plant used in the company's trade but held outside the company where the owner of the asset is the controlling shareholder. If the trading property is held by a non-controlling director, no BPR would be available. Thus there's a strong incentive for you to retain a controlling shareholding.

However, if the property was owned by the company, its value would be reflected in the value of the company's shares, 100% BPR would be available. Where it's feasible you could gift the property to the company with CGT holdover relief being claimed, although a gift to a company does not qualify as a PET, i.e. doesn't leave your estate after seven years. However, a transfer of value or gift could probably be avoided by transferring the property in exchange for shares. A CGT liability might then arise as holdover relief is not available but may be manageable given the availability of your business asset taper relief on the property.

21.4.4. BPR example

Example

Alan owns 35% of the shares in the company. These are valued at £500,000. His wife Gina owns 20%. The company's net assets of £1.6m include surplus cash of £200,000. Alan also owns the business premises worth £230,000 which he lets to the company.

If he were to die, what would be included in his estate for business assets and what BPR is due?

	£
1. Share value	*500,000*
Exclude value of excepted assets	
£500,000 x (£200,000/£1,600,000)	*(62,500)*
	437,500
BPR at 100%	*(437,500)*
Share value to be included in Alan's estate for IHT	*Nil*
2. Property value	*230,000*
BPR at 50% *(Adding Gina's shares as related property, Alan controls the company)*	*(115,000)*
Property value to be included in Alan's estate for IHT	*115,000*
3. Total value to be included in Alan's estate for IHT	
Share value attributable to excepted assets (see above)	*62,500*
Property value	*115,000*
	177,500

21.5. TRANSFERRING SHARES DURING YOUR LIFETIME

If you want to transfer shares to your children or other members of your family, this can basically be done in one of two ways. Shares could be transferred on a phased basis as you approach retirement. Such transfers will qualify as PETs for IHT purposes and CGT business asset holdover relief should normally be available provided neither you nor your spouse can benefit.

TAX BREAK

The effect of a holdover election is to pass the contingent CGT liability to the new shareholder(s).

However, be aware that as the transfer is a PET, if you die within seven years an IHT charge could arise on it.

TAX BREAK

Where IHT becomes payable, BPR will be available if the conditions for it are satisfied, both at the time of the original transfer and at the time of death.

21.6.   SHARES YOU TRANSFER ON DEATH

You could retain your shares (or most of them) until death. Normally the shares would pass to the children etc. free of IHT due to the availability of 100% BPR. The children will also inherit the shares at their market value at the date of death for CGT purposes (and do not therefore take over the contingent CGT liability in the shares which would have occurred had the shares been transferred before death).

The combination of absolute exemption from IHT and CGT provides a persuasive argument for holding onto shares until death. This of course assumes that the 100% BPR exemption will remain intact.

TAX BREAK

If your family plans to sell their shares shortly after death, there will be no claw-back of BPR and there should be little or no CGT.

TAX BREAK

If there's a possibility the company may be sold, consider giving away some shares twelve months before this to enable your children to maximise their entrepreneurs' relief. As a PET for IHT, BPR would protect the shares from tax on a death in seven years, provided the children have not sold their shares at that stage, or having done so invested the proceeds in replacement BPR assets.

21.7.   UNWANTED SHARES

A keyman insurance policy may be taken out to provide a much needed cash sum for the company in the event of your death. The company may use these funds to buy back your shares on death so as to leave cash for your spouse and other dependants.

TAX BREAK

However, there must be no binding contract to buy back the shares since this would lose you 100% BPR. A simple call option granted to the company should achieve the same result without any loss of BPR.

Alternatively, consider nominating (at the discretion of the pension fund trustees) the tax-free "death-in-service" amount of a pension policy in favour of a family trust (perhaps including the surviving spouse). The sum could then be used to purchase from the surviving spouse any non-liquid assets left to them in the will, such as shares in your company.

21.8. PLANNING POINTS FOR YOUR WILL

It's important to get the basic aspects right, such as ensuring that your will is properly drawn up and is regularly reviewed to take account of changes in your circumstances. Where you have assets in different countries it may be desirable to have a concurrent "overseas" will, as well as one dealing with your main assets.

Your will can play a very important IHT planning role. The most significant points are to: **(1)** make sure that you and your spouse make full use of your respective NRBs and; **(2)** your BPR entitlements are maximised.

NRB. Don't waste the NRB, for example, by leaving your entire estate to your spouse, thereby saving IHT at 40% on the second death. If you are not certain of the destination or value of assets likely to be transferred within your NRB, then use a nil-rate band discretionary trust. The beneficiaries of such a trust could be, for example, your surviving spouse and the children. The trust makes distributions in accordance with a letter of wishes from you.

BPR assets. Adopt a similar strategy in relation to your BPR eligible shares and any other BPR qualifying assets. Don't leave them to your surviving spouse. Leave them directly to your children or through an appropriate trust (with the surviving spouse being included as one of the beneficiaries).

Appropriate life assurance arrangements should also be in place to cover potential IHT liabilities which can't be mitigated by planning.

TAX BREAK

Life insurance premiums can normally be paid for the benefit of other members of the family free of IHT, usually under the normal expenditure out of income rule or annual exemption. The benefits of the policy should be held on trust for the beneficiaries so they don't form part of your estate.

Keep within the NRB

- IHT is payable if the sum of your assets at death and the gifts you made in the seven years before death exceeds £325,000 (the NRB). However, there are many gifts and transfers you can make each year, which enable you to avoid IHT
- you can give away almost any amount as long as it is seen to be normal expenditure from your income, is not manifestly from capital, and is capable of being repeated year on year
- where one spouse dies and does not use their NRB to make tax-free bequests to other members of the family, the unused amount can be transferred and used by the second spouse's estate on their death.

Business property relief (BPR)

- BPR applies to all shareholdings including non-voting and preference in unquoted trading companies. These are completely exempt from IHT both on lifetime transfers and on death. To qualify for BPR you need to have held your shareholding for at least two years prior to the transfer/ death
- your shares will not qualify for BPR if you company's business consists mainly or wholly in the dealing of securities, stock and shares or land and buildings. If the predominant activity is trading, then BPR is given on the entire value of the company's shares
- the Taxman can also restrict the BPR on your company shares if the company has excepted assets in its balance sheet. If you have significant cash balances, regularly review them and note in board minutes what future business related-use is intended with these funds
- consider retaining shares in the family/owner-managed company to obtain complete exemption from IHT on death.

Lifetime transfers of shares

- lifetime transfers to the next generation are usually tax-free, but the donee takes on deferred CGT liability.

Unwanted shares

- take out keyman or shareholders' protection insurance to provide a cash sum for your company in the event of your death. It can then use these funds to buy back your shares on death so as to provide cash for your spouse and other dependants. However, there must be no binding contract to buy back the shares since this would lose your 100% BPR. A simple call (to buy your shares) option granted to the company will achieve what you want without any loss of BPR.

KEY POINTS

Update your will

- consider sensible will drafting to maximise use of available NRB and BPR. In many cases it will be beneficial to leave shares and other assets qualifying for BPR via a trust (which could include the surviving spouse as one of the beneficiaries).

CHAPTER 22

Selling your company

22.1. INTRODUCTION

What would you do if you were presented with an opportunity to secure the sale of your company (or one of the companies in your group) at an acceptable price? Which existing tax breaks can maximise your post-tax proceeds?

The only tax you should really be concerned about on any profit on disposal is Capital Gains Tax (CGT). Directors who sell/dispose of the whole or part of the shares in a trading company, in which they have a qualifying interest, now need to factor in the availability of entrepreneurs' relief (ER) into their Capital Gains Tax planning. The new ER can apply when you sell part or all of the shares in your own company, subject to a gains cap of £2 million. The capital gain will be reduced to 5/9ths of the full gain, making the effective CGT rate 10% (5/9 x 18%).

22.2. TIMING THE SALE

The sale of your business will involve a disposal for CGT purposes. The date of the disposal for CGT will be the point at which you enter into an unconditional contract, not the date of completion. Under self-assessment you are liable to pay your CGT bill on the sale by January 31 following the tax year in which the sale is made.

TAX BREAK

If you are close to a tax year-end, consider deferring the date of disposal until after April 6 as this will delay the payment of the tax by one year.

22.3. SALE OF ASSETS AND TRADE

22.3.1. Double tax charge

The proceeds from the sale of the business will be subject to Corporation Tax (CT). If you need the cash from the sale, a further tax liability arises on the extraction of the net proceeds from your company.

22.3.2. Apportionment of proceeds

The tax payable by your company will depend on the nature of each asset and the consideration that has been attributed to each one. It's important to achieve a sensible allocation of the total price paid for the business amongst the various individual assets and this needs to be specified in the sale agreement.

TIP

If your company has unused trading losses which would be lost on cessation, absorb them by allocating higher values to assets that will produce additional trading receipts, such as trading stock or plant or machinery which would produce a balancing charge.

TIP

Place a realistic value on the business's books and records. The value of each individual file, book etc. is below the £6,000 chattel exemption. Given the wide range of the underlying books, files and computer records, it's difficult for the Taxman to argue that the books and records are a set of articles. If they were treated as a set, this would negate the CGT benefit of each individual item being below £6,000.

TIP

Provided you and the purchaser have negotiated the price at arm's length and the allocation has been specified in the sale agreement, the Taxman is unlikely to challenge the apportionment of the total price.

22.3.3. VAT break

VAT may be payable on the sale of assets, whereas the sale of shares is generally exempt. The charge to VAT can be avoided on the transfer of the business as a going concern (TOGC). If the transaction is not a TOGC, VAT will be chargeable on taxable assets, e.g. goodwill, stock, plant and machinery, and on certain commercial land and buildings.

Whether your transaction will qualify as a TOGC depends on the facts and although usually agreed between you and the buyers, the VATman is not bound by your decision.

TIP

Seek to cover your VAT risk with cash or security until confirmation of the VAT position has been obtained. And make sure the contract for sale stipulates that the agreed consideration is exclusive of any VAT which may be payable. Furthermore, have a contractual right included for you to raise a VAT invoice should the VATman subsequently decide that VAT should have been charged on the sale.

22.4. SELLING YOUR SHARES INSTEAD

You can sell your shares for: **(1)** cash; **(2)** shares in the acquiring company; **(3)** loan notes issued by the acquiring company; or **(4)** a mixture of the above. This consideration may be paid immediately on completion or on a deferred basis. Deferred consideration can either be structured as fixed or variable, for example, depending on the future profits of a so-called earn-out arrangement. There's much to be said for receiving all of the consideration up front as a guaranteed amount despite the fact that it will attract an immediate tax liability.

22.4.1. Pre-sale tax breaks

In connection with selling the shares in your company there are a number of other pre-sale strategies that may provide a useful reduction in your tax liability.

Won't the Taxman spot these as being obviously related to the sale? Certain tax-planning techniques may be vulnerable to challenge by the Taxman under the so-called "Furnis v Dawson" principle. The key anti-avoidance cases have established that this principle can only apply where an intermediate tax planning step has been inserted at a time when the ultimate transaction has reached the point of no return. As a general rule, this would be when there's no practical likelihood that the subsequent sale transaction would not happen.

Negotiations for the sale of shares in an unquoted company can often be prolonged and it's not unknown for the transaction to be aborted shortly before the sale was to take place. The implementation of a pre-sale tax mitigation strategy should therefore normally be effective even if it takes place, say, only two or three weeks before the sale agreement is executed.

Take just one more dividend. Pre-sale dividends have traditionally been employed to reduce your effective tax rate to around 25%. They are particularly effective if your capital gain can be substantially eliminated by a dividend out of the company's available distributable profits. With an effective CGT rate of 10% in the current year in most cases, pre-sale cash dividends will generally be disadvantageous since they are likely to increase your overall tax liability.
There are cases where the buyer will require you to extract surplus cash balances held by the company before completion.

Pre-sale dividends will of course continue to be beneficial where you are only entitled to a low level of taper relief. For example, where your company is an investment company.

Rule of thumb. If the shareholders' anticipated CGT rate is expected to materially exceed 25% use a pre-sale dividend to extract profits.

Sack yourself. Many shareholder/directors are strongly tempted by the prospect of a £30,000 tax-free ex-gratia/termination payment prior to the sale. If you did this by arranging for a corresponding deduction in the share price, this would save you CGT at your effective rate.

However, where such payments coincide with the sale of shares, the Taxman's almost automatic reaction is to disallow the payment. This is normally on the basis that the payment is actually a (taxable) dividend or part of the consideration for the sale of shares. Both of which would deny the benefit of the £30,000 exemption in your hands.

If you decide to go down this route, make sure that any ex-gratia payment is not in the agreement for the sale of shares and a board resolution passed indicating that the payment is considered to be in the interests of the company.

TIP

You could make a member of your family a director of the company, pay them a NI-free salary ("director's fees") of up to £100 a week and then in about a year's time they resign "unexpectedly" due to "other commitments". A month after they have resigned the board could decide to pay them a tax-free ex-gratia payment. Making sure, of course, that the board minutes do not say "in appreciation of services".

TIP

An individual lends money to your company but insists on also taking a directorship just to keep an eye on things. Of course, they would have a formal agreement with the company paying loan interest at, say, 5% above base rate. When the loan is repaid they no longer need to be a director and so resign. About a month later the board decide to make an ex-gratia payment which is treated as tax-free. Again, you must make sure that this payment isn't seen as a hidden term of the loan or in appreciation of their services as director.

Retirement catch. If you are approaching retirement age, the official view is that a termination payment represents an unapproved pension benefit. However, in certain circumstances it might be possible to obtain approval from the Taxman's Pension Schemes Office to treat the termination payment as a tax-free pension lump sum.

Special pension contribution. Bearing in mind the risks associated with termination payments it may be more efficient for the company to make a special

---

payment to a pension scheme to enhance your pension rights. The additional pension benefits and the cost of providing them would need to be quantified. If you are near retirement age, the benefits will be quite valuable, for example giving you an increased tax-free lump sum on commutation of the pension.

Strictly between spouses. Your spouse may hold shares in your company to benefit from the spreading of dividends for income tax purposes. However, unless they have worked in the company on a full time basis, their shares are likely to have diluted business asset taper relief for CGT on sale (if they have a non-business asset period).

If you transfer shares to your spouse no CGT liability will arise. And they automatically inherit your base cost and period of ownership of the shares. The taper relief status of the shareholding prior to the transfer is ignored.

TIP

If your spouse doesn't qualify for full business taper relief, it's possible to use the above rule to improve your overall taper relief position. This can be done by unconditionally switching the ownership of the shares well before the final disposal into the hands of the spouse with the most favourable taper relief profile.

In contrast, if you own virtually all the shares, it may be appropriate to save tax by transferring some shares to your spouse, who may be able to use up their annual CGT exemption, and also pay CGT at the lower income tax rate of 20%.

Involving the children. You can gift part of your sale proceeds to your children as part of an IHT planning arrangement. However, if your effective CGT rate is 10%, it makes more sense to retain the shares and then sell them, making any IHT gifts out of post-tax cash received on sale.

As a general rule, transfers to family trusts should be made at the earliest possible time. This will minimise the potential loss of taper relief, especially if the company is to be sold in the short-term.

If you leave the country. Perhaps the most radical step you could contemplate is to establish non-resident status in order to avoid paying UK CGT on the sale of your company. The Taxman's basic condition for this is that you have to leave the country for five years (at least) and take up permanent residence elsewhere.

However, if you're likely to pay an effective CGT rate of around 10% (with the benefit of ER), you should question whether you are willing to endure the inevitable personal and economic upheaval of emigrating for five years to avoid this tax. Your decision would ultimately depend on the absolute amount of tax potentially payable.

Other overseas ideas. The tax advantages of a pre-sale transfer of shares in your company into a non-resident trust and underlying non-resident companies have all but gone. Basically, the Taxman says that to have made disposal at market you are no longer allowed to hold over the gain that arises on those shares. Consequently, the transfer of shares into any form of overseas corporate structure will now produce a tax liability but without the proceeds from an actual sale to fund your tax bill. This also thwarts a pre-sale transfer into offshore bond structures set up by a number of leading merchant banks and insurance companies.

Although offshore corporate/bond structures can still be used for start-up companies where there's as yet no gain on the shares, their attraction has diminished in view of the generous reductions in CGT rates in the UK. Since the majority of shareholders of trading companies can now realise capital gains on their shares at an effective 10% tax rate after just two (post-April 6 1998) years, very few are likely to incur the costs and additional risks associated with overseas structures.

22.5.   THE INHERITANCE TAX ANGLE

Business property relief (BPR) is available on shares in unquoted companies if certain conditions are met, meaning 100% of the market value of those shares escapes Inheritance Tax (IHT). Any business must be owned for two years before the BPR exemption applies. Therefore, if you swap your shares for others in a takeover deal, the BPR clock resets to zero. This means a potential IHT bill at 40% on the value of the sale.

Example

Harry has just sold his company H Ltd to Takeover Ltd for £2m. He received £1m in cash and the balance as a stake in Takeover Ltd. As soon as Harry received cash for his shares the BPR ceased to apply. The sale of Harry's company has increased the IHT bill on his estate by £800,000 (£2m x 40%) if he dies within two years of the sale.

Tɪᴘ

Take out life assurance cover for the first two years to provide the funds to pay the IHT bill. However, there are other steps you can take to mitigate this.

If the new shares can be treated as replacements for the old shares, then the BPR ownership clock does not stop, meaning you get 100% relief on the new shares. We recommend taking specialist advice to check if these are replacement shares, since this is a complex area where both shares (old and new) have a number of conditions to meet.

If the replacement shares route is not available, consider leaving the new shares in your will to your spouse. No IHT is payable on this transfer between spouses and the surviving spouse is treated as if they had owned the shares for the whole period.

If you transfer the shares to your spouse before death, the ownership clock is restarted and so the spouse must wait two years before the shares qualify for BPR.

If, for some reason, the spouse exemption is not available, you could reinvest the proceeds from the sale into shares of unquoted trading companies. You are then putting your money back into an IHT-exempt asset. Shares issued under the Enterprise Investment Scheme (EIS) qualify, as will any trading in an unquoted company. If a share is listed on Alternative Investment Market (AIM) it's unquoted. However, remember the two-year qualifying period, and take out life assurance to cover the risk of having to pay the IHT in the intervening time.

TAX BREAK

Check to see if the shares qualify as a replacement. This way the BPR period is continuous. If not and you have to wait two years to regain BPR, take out life assurance to cover yourself in the meantime.

22.6. USEFUL WARRANTIES AND INDEMNITIES

Get your advisor to negotiate the tax warranties in detail to ensure that you're not exposed to the actions or omissions of the buyer after sale. They should seek to negotiate that the warranties and indemnities do not apply where events occur after completion which are outside your control.

Consider seeking warranties from the buyer for actions by the purchaser after the completion of the sale that may adversely affect your tax position. Such circumstances would include the failure to account for and pay VAT for which it became liable whilst still included under your VAT registration.

22.7. ENTREPRENEURS' RELIEF (ER)

22.7.1. The basic tax break

ER can apply when you sell part or all of the shares in your own company, subject to a gains cap of £2 million. The capital gain will be reduced to 5/9ths of the full gain, making the effective CGT rate 10% (5/9 x 18%).

Example

You sell the shares in your company for a gain of £450,000. ER reduces the gain to £250,000 (5/9 x £450,000). The tax due is £45,000 (18% x £250,000); an effective rate of 10% on the full gain of £450,000. You can also deduct your annual exemption (£10,100 for 2010/11), and any capital losses from the taxable gain to reduce your tax bill even further.

There's no minimum age limit on the ER, so you don't have to "retire" when you sell your business to qualify. But there is a lifetime limit of £2 million of gains that can be subject to the relief. This means you can make a number of gains totalling £2 million over several years, and claim ER on them all. Any gains in excess of £2 million will be taxed at the full 18%.

Example

David owned a freehold sports shop and a leasehold shoe shop. He sells the businesses in May 2010 and May 2011 respectively, and makes the following gains and losses:

2010/11	£	£
Sports shop - sold May 2010		
Freehold		720,000
Goodwill		400,000
Net gain		1,120,000
Entrepreneurs' relief 4/9 £1,120,000		(497,777)
Taxable gain		622,223

2011/12	£	£
Shoe shop - sold May 2011		
Leasehold		(40,000)
Goodwill		920,000
Net gain		880,000
Lifetime limit for entrepreneur's relief	2,000,000	
Gains used in an ER claim previously	(1,120,000)	
Available to use against 2011/12 gain	880,000	
Entrepreneur's relief 4/9 x £800,000		(391,111)
Taxable gain		488,889

However, the Taxman has said that he has no plans to monitor the £2 million limit himself. It will be up to you to keep a record of how much of your lifetime limit you use up over the years.

22.7.2. Material disposal

In order to qualify for ER there must be a qualifying business disposal:

- a material disposal of a business

- a disposal of business assets

- an associated disposal.

A material disposal is defined as a disposal of:

- the whole or part of the business - where the individual has owned the business asset for the year leading up to the date of disposal

- assets in use for the purposes of the business where the business ceases to be carried on, if the disposal is made within three years and the individual owned the business for the year preceding cessation

- shares or securities of a company where either of two conditions are met.

A disposal of shares. The two conditions for shares in companies are:

Condition "A". Throughout the year proceeding the disposal: **(1)** the company is the individual's personal company; **(2)** the company is a trading company or holding company of a trading group; and **(3)** the individual is an officer or employee of the company (or one or more companies that are members of a group).

Condition "B". This is satisfied where the company has, within three years preceding disposal, ceased to be either a trading company or a member of a trading group. The tests laid down by condition "A" must be satisfied throughout the year preceding the cessation.

For the purposes of ER, an individual's personal company is one in which they hold 5% of the ordinary share capital of the company and have at least 5% of the voting rights of the company.

A trading company group is defined as one that carries on trading activities and does not carry on other activities to a substantial extent. This is the same condition as applied for taper relief purposes.

22.7.3. Offset other losses

Once the losses on the disposal of the same business have been aggregated with losses for that business, any of the losses brought forward or arising in the same tax year are set off against the residue of the gain after ER has been applied.

Example

Sarah gives 25% of the shares in her personal company to her daughter in June 2010, making a gain based on the market value of £270,000. Sarah also made a loss of £100,000 in February 2009 on the disposal of quoted shares. The loss was not used in 2009/10.

2010/11	£
Gain on gift	270,000
Entrepreneurs' relief 4/9 x £270,000	(120,000)
Taxable gain	150,000
Loss brought forward	(100,000)
Taxable gain before annual exemption	50,000

This good news is that the losses have been relieved at the full rate of CGT of 18% not the ER effective rate of 10%.

22.7.4. Actually make a claim for ER

ER must be claimed by the individual who makes the gain; although in the case of gains made by trustees, the claim must be signed by both the trustees and the beneficiary. You will normally make the claim on your tax return for the tax year in which the gain arose. If no tax return has been issued to you or your return has already been submitted, you can make a claim by letter to the Taxman.

The claim has to be made by the first anniversary of January 31 following the tax year in which the gain arose. For example, if you make a gain in 2010/11 you have until January 31 2013 to make a claim for ER. However, you can withdraw your claim within the same period.

22.8. BEFORE YOU DISPOSE OF YOUR SHARES

22.8.1. Maintaining personal company status

It's a condition for obtaining ER on a share sale that the company in question is your personal company, with a minimum 5% interest. So trying to fragment holdings below this threshold is pointless. Instead, people who fall below the 5% threshold should do some judicious topping up of their holdings to get them above the limit, provided this makes commercial sense, of course.

Example

Gavin and Stacey are married and jointly own 9.4% of the ordinary shares of Lush Ltd. They are each treated as owning 4.7% of Lush Ltd, so the company will not qualify as their personal company. If each acquire a further 0.3% of the ordinary shares in their sole names Lush Ltd will qualify as their personal company, but they both need to meet the employment requirement for their disposals of shares in Lush Ltd to qualify for ER.

Warning. Remember that any attempt to give people further shares might have other tax consequences. There may be a disposal for CGT purposes or the value of shares may count as employment income.

22.8.2. Beware of issuing new shares

If your company has different classes of share capital, some of which have limited rights, you may need to change it if you want to maximise your entitlement to ER. This is because to satisfy the 5% test, you must have entitlement to **both** 5% of the votes and 5% of the voting share capital. For example, you might want to let your employees/junior members of your family participate in the income and capital of the business, but do not want them to have a say in how the company is run and may have issued non-voting shares. These employees will not be entitled to ER.

TIP

There is nothing, however, to say that you must have voting rights pro rata to your holdings, just that you should have at least 5%. So in this situation you might consider amending the voting rights of different holdings. This could increase the availability of ER on any future sale. Handing out voting rights could trigger an immediate tax charge to the extent that those rights have some value, although the right to have 5% of the votes of a private company may not in fact be worth all that much.

Take care with new issues of shares, since they will dilute everyone's holding and may depress some shareholders below the crucial 5% threshold. Conversely, purchase of own shares by your company may have an added benefit of pushing shareholders above the 5% point and giving them a new entitlement to the relief. Whenever such transactions take place, recalculate the entitlement to ER.

22.8.3. Keep working for your company

To qualify for ER you must be either an officer or employee of the company. However, if your company is a member of a trading group, being employed by one of the other companies in that group qualifies.

Example

Dewy has worked for Tyres R Us Ltd for 20 years and owns 7% of the ordinary shares and voting rights. He also owns 5% of the ordinary shares of Best Brakes R Us Ltd , but he does not work for that company. The remaining shares in both companies are held by a holding company Autoparts Ltd. When Tyres R Us and Brakes R Us are sold, Dewy will qualify for ER in respect of his shareholding in both companies, as he has satisfied the employment requirement of either working for the actual company or another company of the same trading group.

TIP

There's no requirement to work full-time or even for a minimum number of hours to qualify for ER. There's also no requirement for the shareholder to be paid, however, without a contract of employment it might be difficult to show that an individual who received no pay was employed. The requirements of the National Minimum Wage will normally require the company to make some payment to all its employees. Therefore, it may be worth bringing shareholders onto the payroll to increase entitlement to ER.

Even so, any employment should have commercial substance and an essentially made-up job would probably not withstand close scrutiny by the Taxman. Although not a strict statutory requirement, it would be prudent to make sure any employment that purports to exist be properly documented.

Note. Being an office holder of the company also counts for these purposes. A statutory director is an office holder, as is a company secretary. It's true that company law no longer technically requires that there be a company secretary but retaining this post does give opportunity for someone to fill it and claim ER on the back of it. Non-executive directors count as officers but shadow directors do not.

Key point. Whether an individual was an officer of the company (director or company secretary) should easily be confirmed by the records held at Companies House. Therefore, make sure officers are properly appointed in accordance with company law and correctly registered at Companies House.

Trustees need to get involved too. ER will also be available to trustees on disposals. The conditions largely apply to the beneficiary of the trust, such as the "officer and employee" condition, and the relief is available up to the £2 million limit between the beneficiary and the trustees. So if a claim is made by the trustees in respect of a shareholding acquired pre-April 2008, on a disposal after that date, then the beneficiary will be treated as having used some or all of their lifetime limit.

22.9. ASSOCIATED DISPOSAL TAX BREAK

Essentially, you need to know about this if you own an asset personally that is used by your company. The classic examples include keeping the trading premises in your own name and renting it to your company to use, or you own the intellectual property rights to a product which your company sells and you charge a licence fee for using it.

TAX BREAK

If you dispose of the asset used by your company at around the same time as selling your shares in your company, then the gain on that asset will also qualify for ER as an associated disposal; provided certain conditions are met of course.

KEY POINTS

- there are two ways in which your company may be sold - selling the shares or selling the assets, and either liquidating the company or keeping it and distributing the dividends from its subsequent income. The most difficult aspect of the sale negotiation is usually reconciling your tax interests and those of the buyers
- normally your major objective will be to maximise the net sale proceeds from the sale of your company, whilst minimising the number of warranties you have to give, any long-term commitments, and the dependence of the purchase price on future performance of the target after sale
- if you transfer shares to your spouse no CGT liability will arise, and they automatically inherit your base cost and period of ownership of the shares. The taper relief status of the shareholding prior to the transfer is ignored
- when selling shares in a family company with significant profits, the Taxman might argue that the increased share value should be taxed as income and not as part of the capital gain on the shares
- get your advisor to consider the anti-avoidance legislation and to make application for clearances. And where there is deferred consideration, get them to check that the deal meets the conditions for deferral of your CGT liability and to make that election (within the time limit).

CHAPTER 23

Year-end planning for directors

23.1.   WHY IS TIMING IMPORTANT?

Having decided on which tax breaks to use, there remains the question of which order to arrange them in.

The Taxman's PAYE system is waiting in the wings to take income tax and NI from you on a monthly (or possibly weekly) basis. For you, timing means getting your hands on your money as quickly as possible, whilst also trying to delay the date you'll have to pay over the related tax for as long as possible. This gives you the opportunity to put the money you will ultimately pay across to good use, e.g. using it to reduce private borrowings and save on interest charges. For example, this could mean delaying the start of a particular tax break until the beginning of the next tax year and using others first during the current one.

23.2.   THAT APRIL 5 DATE

The tax year coming to a close on April 5 is your last chance to review your position to uncover any unused tax breaks. Remember, if you're entitled to any allowances or tax breaks, make sure you use them or you'll lose them once the tax year ends.

It's also a good time to consider possible actions to mitigate the 50% tax rate if this will apply to you. However, as with any personal finance decisions, great care should be taken before choosing which course of action to follow, so seeking expert advice is essential.

Here are a few subjects under which you and your tax advisor can marshal your thoughts.

23.2.1. Personal allowances

Maximise income tax rate bands

TAX BREAK

Make a gift to a spouse to make use of their personal allowance (£6,475 for 2010/11) and basic/lower rate band (£37,400 for 2010/11). Taxpayers with an income over £150,000 pay tax at 50%, a gift to a spouse whose top rate of tax is 40% will also be effective.

Capital Gains Tax (CGT)

TAX BREAK

Make use of the annual exemption (AE). For 2010/11 this is £10,100 for each individual, including children. If already used, you can consider delaying the disposal until 2011/12.

Inheritance Tax (IHT)

TAX BREAK

Make use of the AE for 2010/11 of £3,000 each for husband and wife, plus any unused balance from 2009/10, and the small exemption of £250 in relation to individuals. Also, make use of this tax year's £325,000 nil-rate band (NRB).

Individual Savings Accounts (ISAs)

TAX BREAK

Make use of the yearly ISA allowance: £5,100 for a cash ISA and £10,200 for a stocks and shares ISA. The increased limits are not just for the over 50s.

23.2.2. Pensions

It's worth considering making a pension contribution to get a tax break. However, with the many changes to pension tax legislation over the last few years, great care should be taken, as higher rate relief may not be available.

From April 6 2011, higher rate tax relief on pension contributions will be gradually phased out for individuals with gross incomes of at least £150,000, so that for those with gross incomes of more than £180,000 tax relief will be restricted to the basic rate only.

Anti-forestalling measures were introduced with immediate effect from April 22 2009 imposing a special annual allowance charge in 2009/10 and 2010/11 on certain contributions in excess of an individual's normal ongoing savings pattern. From December 9 2009 the level of relevant income was dropped to take effect from £130,000.

For those making contributions less frequently than quarterly, the special annual allowance may be up to a maximum of £30,000. For example, an individual who made a relevant single one-off contribution in 2006/7 of £75,000 will have a special annual allowance for 2009/10 and 2010/11 of £25,000 (i.e. £75,000/3).

23.2.3. The 50% tax rate

There are some simple steps which may assist in mitigating the 50% tax rate to some extent, although as with all planning, the overall commercial picture must be considered as well as the tax issues:

- if accelerating income to the 2010/11 tax year will mean that it's taxed at 40% rather than 50%, albeit with a cash flow disadvantage of having to pay tax one year earlier, this is worth considering

- closing a bank account in 2010/11 will mean that interest becomes payable in that year

- exercising unapproved share options will trigger an income tax charge in 2010/11

- bringing forward deductions to 2010/11 will have the same effect. Plus, a director with an income in 2010/11 between £100,000 and approximately £113,000 will have a marginal rate of 60% due to the tapered withdrawal of the personal allowance, so deductions of this nature are particularly beneficial

- wrappers, such as investment bonds, are useful, as they allow 5% withdrawals made annually without triggering a charge to tax, and the bond can be cashed at a later date when the individual is no longer a 50% taxpayer.

23.3.   KEY DATES FOR YOUR COMPANY

Your company pays Corporation Tax (CT) on its profits nine months after its year-end. By putting tax breaks in place before the year-end you should be in a position to reduce that CT bill. Otherwise you'll have to wait, say, another 21 months for it to have an impact. Why 21 months? That's another twelve-month accounting period of your company plus nine months before a CT bill is due again. Broadly, the action your company needs to do falls into the following points in time, which are before:

1. Its year-end.

2. The accounts for that year are finalised.

3. Nine months have elapsed after the year-end.

23.3.1. Before your company's year-end

During the last two months of your company's financial year consider:

Pension contributions. Although you didn't select it as one of your preferred methods of profit extraction, consider whether the company can afford to pay a contribution into your pension plan. If it pays this before the end of its financial year this will reduce any CT it has to pay in nine months' time.

Assets for your use. If the company wants to lend you any assets to use, e.g. a laptop computer, it will get an earlier tax deduction for their acquisition cost if it acquires them before its year-end, rather than shortly afterwards.

23.3.2. Before the accounts are finalised

As part of the final adjustments to your company's annual accounts before they are approved and signed off by the directors, consider:

Bonuses. Making a provision for directors' and other employees' bonuses to reduce the profit and hence the CT payable on those accounts.

Expenses. Including accruals in the accounts for any expenses due to you that were unpaid at the year-end.

23.3.3. Before the nine-month deadline

Salaries and bonuses. In order for your company to get a deduction for the salary and bonus-related figures included in its accounts, make sure that any tax or NI due on those has been paid within nine months of that year-end.

Final dividend. You've taken interim dividends so far. After the accounts have been finalised it's time to consider taking a final dividend out of the company. Remember, only the shareholders of the company can approve a final dividend so the date of this will be linked to when you hold the company's Annual General Meeting.

23.3.4. Board minutes

The Articles of Association require the shareholders to agree on major aspects of company policy such as directors' remuneration. Usually this is evidenced by voting on a resolution or two at a company's general meeting. However, in practice, the company will pay amounts to directors before this meeting happens. You should therefore record, in a director's board minute, the level of, e.g., bonus which has been agreed for the year, before it is taken.

23.3.5. Director's loan account

The director/shareholder could leave what they are entitled to within the company, so that the company credits the relevant amount to their director's loan account. It's then available for them to draw at any time they want. However, you will be taxed as if the company had given you a cheque on the date it's put into your director's loan account.

23.4. WHEN WILL YOUR COMPANY GET A TAX DEDUCTION?

A company pays Corporation Tax (CT) on its profits (for an accounting period) nine months after its year-end. The starting point to calculate how much CT it will pay is the profit before tax figure shown in its final accounts. If you can get the cost of your tax break included in those accounts as an expense, it will reduce the CT bill sooner rather than later.

If the company has an obligation to pay the sum at its year-end, then it can provide for that expense when finalising its accounts for that year - even if it hasn't paid the money across yet.

The main exceptions to this rule to watch out for are:

Salary and bonus. If you make a provision for salary or bonus in the year-end accounts of your company, the PAYE due on these must be paid within nine months of that year-end. If it isn't, then these get added back to the company's profits by the Taxman, which will in turn increase the company's CT bill.

Pension contributions. It's the amount of pension premium paid by the company before its year-end that counts, not what it's obliged to pay. For example:

> *Example*
>
> *If the company draws up its accounts to March 31 2011, any pension contribution for 2010/11 must be paid by March 31 to be set against the profits made in the 2011 set of accounts. A contribution is therefore an ideal way to reduce the taxable profit of the company before the financial year-end has passed.*

Royalties. The payment of a royalty to you will reduce the amount of CT paid by the company on its total profits for its accounting period, but it can't be used to turn a profit into a loss or increase tax losses. If the company has no taxable profits, the royalty payment is carried forward to be deducted in the next accounting period.

Benefits-in-kind. If you plan to take tax efficient benefits-in-kind, your company will have to pay the Taxman, by July 6 each year, employers' NI (currently at the rate of 12.8%) on their value. This relates to the tax year not the company year, i.e. benefits made available to you between April 6 in one year and April 5 in the next.

Dividends. Your need for cash may dictate the regular payment of dividends by your company to you. These are known as interim dividends whose typical timing is quarterly, though there is an increasing fashion for monthly dividends to be paid. A final divided can also be paid to you once the reserves for the year are known (from the final accounts), but payment of this is linked to the company's Annual General Meeting. The point is that for either an interim or final dividend to be validly

Year-end planning for directors

paid requires distributable reserves. If the company has these, then it can pay that dividend. At the time a dividend is declared the company's financial records must be adequate to demonstrate this is the case. Reliable management accounts will normally satisfy this requirement.

Interim dividends are treated by the Taxman as "made" when cheques are issued to you (as a shareholder) or when funds are at your disposal by way of an accounting entry in the company's books, e.g. posted as a credit to your director's loan account.

KEY POINTS

- when you start using a new tax break there can be up to a 21-month delay in it affecting your personal tax bill. For example, if you start charging your company a monthly rent on April 6 2011, then you won't have a tax bill to pay on that until January 31 2013. Thereafter you'll be asked to make payments on account of your total tax bill (provided it exceeds £500) each July and January as long as you have this source of income

- delaying tax bills means you'll need to remember to organise payment of them at some future date. If the money isn't there when it's eventually due, you might need to resort to another round of profit extraction, sufficient to put you in funds to settle your account with the Taxman

- if you're going to pay regular interim dividends, you'll need accurate quarterly management accounts to avoid the risk of them being classed as illegal dividends (where the dividends exceed the final profits available for distribution).